V

A clinical biochemist
on Vitamin C, exam
and shows how to

VITAMIN C
Enemy of the Common Cold

by

LEONARD MERVYN
B.Sc., Ph.D., F.R.S.C.

NATURE'S WAY

THORSONS PUBLISHERS LIMITED
Wellingborough, Northamptonshire

First published 1981
Second Impression 1982

British Library Cataloguing in Publication Data

Mervyn, Leonard
  Vitamin C.
  1. Vitamin C
  2. Vitamins in human nutrition
  I. Title
  612'.399   QP772.A8

  ISBN 0-7225-0717-8

Printed and bound in Great Britain by
Richard Clay (The Chaucer Press) Limited,
Bungay, Suffolk.

CONTENTS

INTRODUCTION

The presence of some factor in food that prevented and cured the dreaded disease scurvy had been suspected for centuries, yet it was not until the 1750s that citrus fruits were proved to be a rich source of this factor. It took a further two hundred years before the specific substance was isolated and characterized as ascorbic acid, or vitamin C. Yet, even today, some fifty years after its discovery, this essential vitamin still leaves many questions unanswered.

What, for example, is the optimum intake of vitamin C? Clinical studies have indicated the minimum requirements to prevent scurvy, but there could be a much higher over-all need to ensure optimum health. The required intake could be three, ten, twenty or even a hundred times more if various authorities are to be believed. The simple truth is that no one knows. The only agreement is that the U.K. suggested minimum intake of 30mg per day is too low. At a recent gathering of all the experts in vitamin C research, at the University of Warwick, it was generally accepted that this official figure needs to be increased. Is the metabolism of Britons so different from that of Americans and Russians that we require only one half or one third respectively of their suggested minimum daily intake?

How do vitamin C requirements vary amongst individuals? The needs for the vitamin will differ because of genetic, environmental, lifestyle and age variations amongst members of any population. How can we determine who needs more than others? Should we not aim for diets that will satisfy the vitamin C intake of those at the upper end of the scale, be it 500mg or more per day? The table in Chapter 2 shows that these intakes are covered in good quality diets.

What happens when a person is on a long-term sub-optimal intake of vitamin C? What are the signs and symptoms, if any, of the conditions associated with just sufficient ascorbic acid to prevent scurvy but not enough to satisfy demands for optimum health? There must be a grey area in between these two levels of intake. Some researchers believe that a lifetime of barely sufficient vitamin C in the diet can lead to many of the conditions associated with old age such as heart disease, arthritis, arteriosclerosis, hypertension, eye problems and perhaps even cancer. It is easy to hypothesize on these possibilities, but far more difficult to prove them.

How relevant is supplementary vitamin C in treating diseases such as arthritis, viral infections like the common cold and influenza, iron-deficiency anaemia and some tumours? Will the vitamin in high doses accelerate wound healing, the mending of bone fractures and the healing of ulcers in the gastro-intestinal tract? There is some evidence that vitamin C may be beneficial in all these conditions, but hard facts are still tantalizingly vague. When one group of researchers is unable to repeat the positive results of another group, what are the reasons? Is it dosage, selection of patients, the protocol of the clinical trial, varying criteria of assessing benefits, or simply the fact that these researchers are studying the effects of just one nutrient, vitamin C, without reference to others that may be associated with it?

The ultimate question, however, must be how safe are these relatively high intakes of vitamin C? When we look at what our fellow consumers of the vitamin, the primates, take in their daily diets in the wild, it is obvious that our intakes are extremely low in com-parison. The species who are able to make their own vitamin C also have body levels pro rata far in excess of those in man. None of these animals appears to suffer from an overdose of the vitamin. Yet we are regaled with what may happen to us on high intakes of ascorbic acid, based usually on anecdotal evidence from one or two individual cases. This type of evidence would be ignored if it were put forward as reasons for suggesting the benefits of vitamin C, yet it is happily accepted as a clear-cut reason for not taking high intakes of the vitamin.

The question of toxicity of vitamin C is resolved in Chapter 6 where the results of clinical and scientific research are discussed. These give a much clearer indication of just how safe the vitamin is when it is taken in doses that are both effective and sensible.

There are thus many questions that must be asked about this versatile vitamin, and the following chapters present the evidence so that readers can make up their own minds. Health is of concern to everyone, so the book concentrates on how vitamin C may contribute to a full and active life. What it does not do is describe in detail the other attributes of ascorbic acid as a food preservative and a dough improver. Vast quantities of ascorbic acid are sold to the food and baking industries for these purposes. In addition, for example, brewers use ascorbic acid as a clarifier, and the meat curing industry find it helps preserve the natural colour of their products. When vitamin C is added to flour at the rate of only 75 parts per million (i.e. about 100mg to 1.5kg or 3 lb of flour), it acts as a natural and safe dough improver to such an extent that only one rising is required. Much of the vitamin is destroyed during the subsequent baking process, but the quality of the loaf is greatly improved. In this respect ascorbic acid is acting as a weak organic acid rather than as a vitamin, but its natural quality makes it superior to the usual chemical additives accepted by the baking trade and it now has the official blessing of government authorities.

CHAPTER 1

THE PROPERTIES OF VITAMIN C AND OUR DAILY NEEDS

Vitamin C is unique amongst the vitamins because most species of animals are able to synthesize it. Human beings share with the primates (monkeys, apes etc.), the guinea-pig, the Indian fruit-eating bat and a bird known as the red-vented bulbul the dubious distinction of not having the ability to synthesize the vitamin and so needing to obtain it ready-made from their food. This deficiency is the result of some long past mutation in the evolution of man and the other species, which resulted in the loss of a particular enzyme, required for the final step in the biosynthesis of ascorbic acid. Glucose is the starting material in the series of biological conversions that results in a substance called L-gulonolactone which in turn gives rise to ascorbic acid. It is this final stage that cannot be performed by man and the other species unable to make the vitamin.

When human beings, the primates and the guinea-pig are deprived of vitamin C they develop a disease called scurvy. Amongst all the vitamin-deficiency diseases known to us today, that of scurvy must rank as the oldest to be described. Mention is made of it in the Old Testament and in the writings of the Roman patriarch Pliny the Elder, who saw it in his travels during the first years of the first century A.D. It was not until the advent of sailing ships that the disease became the scourge that sailors came to dread.

The galleys of the Egyptians, Greeks and Romans rarely left sight of land so that fresh food was always available to the crews. The exciting exploratory voyages of the fourteenth and fifteenth centuries could be undertaken only because of the development of ships efficiently propelled by sail. Much greater distances could be covered, and often food stores loaded at the outset of voyages had to last many months. Consequently the staple diet of sailors at that time consisted of foods that would keep, such as hard biscuits, salt beef and salt pork all of which are practically devoid of vitamin C. Little wonder, then, that if fresh provisions were not available at ports of call, a deficiency of vitamin C soon resulted.

The sufferings of scurvy were not confined to seamen. Prolonged sieges during land warfare often gave rise to the disease on both sides. Winter campaigns denied access to fresh fruit and vegetables to marauding armies with the consequent low intake of vitamin C. The seasonal variation in the quantity of vitamin C-rich foods eaten also meant winters of misery for civilian populations.

It was not until the introduction of the potato and other root vegetables into Europe that people had access to a food that could supply them with vitamin C when the leaf vegetables and fruits were not available. Workhouses and prisons were notorious as places where the incidence of scurvy was high, mainly due to the poor diets given to the inmates. Even today, the vitamin C levels of some hospital diets, and those of other institutions, creates concern for those spending long periods in such places. Perhaps for this reason alone the practice of taking fresh fruit into patients should be encouraged.

The extent of suffering induced by scurvy on the long voyages 200 or more years ago is difficult to imagine. During the years 1497 and 1498 the Portuguese navigator, Vasco de Gama sailed from Lisbon around the Cape of Good Hope and reached India to establish a new sea route when the old one, via the Mediterranean was denied to the Western world by the Turks. Scurvy claimed the lives of 100 of his 160 men. Ships were often found adrift, with all on board dead from the disease. The navies of the European powers had critical losses in manpower during long months blockading ports or crossing the oceans. A classic example occurred in 1740 when a British Admiral, George Anson, set out with a squadron of six ships and a total crew of 961. Eight months later he arrived at the island of Juan Fernandez off the coast of Chile having lost a total of 626 souls, most of them from scurvy.

Although some captains had discovered the value of citrus fruits in preventing scurvy, poor communications did not give their findings the dissemination they deserved. It was not until 1753 that Dr James Lind, a Scottish naval surgeon, published *A Treatise of the Scurvy* in which he showed conclusively that the disease could be prevented and cured by eating fresh oranges and lemons. His study must rank as the first controlled clinical trial ever undertaken, and deserves to be recorded here.

Twelve sailors, diagnosed as suffering from scurvy, were isolated from the rest of the crew. Two were given a quart of cider per day; two were treated with a popular remedy of the time, called elixir vitriol, consisting of dilute sulphuric acid, ginger, cinnamon and alcohol mixture; two took vinegar three times per day and two of the worst cases were given half-a-pint of sea water daily. Two oranges and a lemon were eaten by two of the patients and the final pair had to subsist on a nutmeg three times a day, plus a concoction of garlic, mustard seed, Peru balsam and gum myrrh. Not surprisingly, only those on fresh fruit were cured and at the end of a mere six days treatment they were able to resume duties.

Dr Lind, however, was very astute and he realized that although the citrus fruits supplied some substance responsible for preventing scurvy, environmental factors such as exposure to cold and wet, drunkenness, foul air and overcrowding also contributed to the development of the disease. Today we would regard such conditions as 'stress', and now we know that stress in many forms can increase the requirements for vitamin C.

As well as proving that fresh fruit was necessary to prevent scurvy, Lind was also responsible for improving the lot of sailors. This combination eventually paved the way for the total eradication of the disease from the naval forces of Britain. When Captain James Cook made his historic voyage from 1772 to 1775, resulting in the discovery of Australia and New Zealand, he was aware of the value of fresh fruit in the diet of his men and not one case of scurvy was recorded.

The Isolation of Vitamin C

Ascorbic acid was isolated from natural sources long before its properties as a vitamin became apparent. In 1922, a Hungarian doctor, Albert Szent-Györgi was studying the reactions that cause the brown pigmentation to appear in apples and bananas as they decay in the presence of air. He found that these fruits, along with cabbage, contain a reducing agent that protects certain compounds in the intact plant from being converted into these brown pigments. Such an agent is known as an anti-oxidant. Paprika, a favourite condiment in his native Hungary, was also found to be a particularly rich source of the same factor. Dr Szent-Györgi later isolated an identical compound from the adrenal glands of animals.

Patient work over the next five years enabled the doctor to extract a total of 25g of this reducing agent which he named hexuronic acid. Fortunately some years earlier in 1907, Doctors Holst and Frölich had found that guinea-pigs were susceptible to scurvy, so a ready-made animal model system was available to test for vitamin C activity. Hence in 1932, Dr Szent-Györgi in Hungary and Drs W. A. Waugh and C. G. King at Columbia University, U.S.A., discovered that the hexuronic acid isolated from plants and animals was able to cure scurvy in guinea-pigs and it was promptly designated vitamin C. Further studies by Dr Szent-Györgi and the British sugar chemist, Professor W. M. Howath, soon characterized the chemical structure of vitamin C, which proved to be a simple sugar. Between them they coined the name ascorbic acid, a condensation of anti-scorbutic acid, meaning preventing scurvy.

The Active Forms of Vitamin C

Ascorbic acid can exist in two forms, the laevo or L-ascorbic acid and the dextro or D-ascorbic acid. Only L-ascorbic acid is active in animals and this is the form in which it occurs in nature. Fortunately, synthetic vitamin C made by a chemist in a laboratory is also the L-form of ascorbic acid and so it too can be utilized by people and animals. Animals that can make their own vitamin C do so by converting glucose into ascorbic acid. Similarly, a chemist starts with glucose and by a series of chemical reactions L-ascorbic acid can be synthesized. Other methods utilize fermentation techniques to produce the vitamin, but no matter from which source ascorbic acid is made, the end-product is biologically active.

Ascorbic acid is a powerful reducing agent and when acting in this way, itself is oxidized to dehydroascorbic acid. Other substances present in the biological system then reconvert dehydroascorbic acid back to ascorbic acid. Both compounds can be equally utilized by the body and either form may be regarded as vitamin C. In its metabolic action vitamin C may be regarded as constantly see-sawing between these two acids, ascorbic and dehydroascorbic. However, further oxidation of dehydroascorbic acid leads to compounds that cannot be re-converted to ascorbic acid and these have no vitamin C activity.

In foods, both ascorbic acid and dehydroascorbic acid occur, but ascorbic acid is the predominant form. For example, in acerola cherry juice each 100g contains 3300mg of ascorbic acid and only 90mg as dehydroascorbic acid. Juice from the camu-camu plum contains a slightly higher proportion of the dehydro acid, 114mg to 2880mg of the ascorbic acid in every 100g. Between five and ten per cent of the vitamin C of most foods is present as dehydroascorbic acid. The terms ascorbic acid and vitamin C may be regarded as synonymous and we may regard dehydro-ascorbic acid as having full vitamin C activity.

What Happens When We Eat Vitamin C?

Vitamin C is absorbed directly from the gastro-intestinal tract into the blood stream. How much is absorbed, depends very much on the amount eaten — with small intakes of up to 250mg some 80 per cent finds its way to the blood. As the intake rises, the extent of absorption diminishes, so with a dose of 2000mg only 50 per cent is absorbed. When 3000mg is eaten at one time, the amount that enters the blood stream is 1200mg. For this reason, it is better to take vitamin C in divided doses since, for example 500mg taken three times per day is more efficiently absorbed than a single 1500mg dose taken once.

Such considerations apply only to conventional tablets, capsules and powder. A high potency single-dose tablet is acceptable if this is of the prolonged-release type. This tablet is manufactured in such a way as to disintegrate slowly in the gut, releasing the vitamin C as it moves down the digestive tract. Hence absorption is sustained, leading to consistent levels of the vitamin in the blood. The prolonged release system is more akin to that which applies when food is eaten, since vitamins can only be released as the food is digested; thus a similar pattern of absorption is

established. The complicated structure of food constituents leads to a built-in prolonged release
mechanism.

The Body Pool of Vitamin C

The amount of vitamin C eaten determines the total
quantity present in the body known as the body pool.
Dr R. E. Hodges in the U.S.A. studied this in 1971,
using volunteers from Iowa State Penitentiary.
Ascorbic acid, containing a tiny amount of radioactive
carbon was given to the volunteers. The potency of this
radioactivity was known, and as this labelled material
became mixed with the existing ascorbic acid in the
prisoners, it became diluted. By counting the radioactivity in the vitamin C after its distribution throughout the body, the total amount present was easily
calculated. The results indicated that with an intake of
75mg of ascorbic acid per day, the average body
content was 1500mg. This dropped to 300mg after
only 55 days on a vitamin C-free diet.

On the U.K. recommended daily intake of 30mg,
the size of the pool would be only 1000mg. Many
researchers believe that the minimum body pool
should be 1500mg, but if saturation of the body tissues
is required, a more desirable pool is 4000mg of the
vitamin. Whether the body should be saturated with
ascorbic acid or not, is the main controversial issue
when official authorities make their recommendations
for a minimal daily intake. There is no hard evidence
either way.

The Iowa study on the long-suffering prison inmates
also indicated that the catabolic rate (rate of utilization
or loss) of vitamin C is about 3 per cent of the body
pool. Hence with a body pool of 1500mg, the rate of
utilization is 45mg per day. As the body pool fell to
300mg, so the rate of loss dropped to less than 9mg per
day, showing that during times of deficiency the body
zealously retains its dwindling reserves of vitamin C.

On the strength of this evidence it is difficult to understand how some authorities still persist in suggesting only 30mg of vitamin C per day as the minimum recommended daily allowance. Common sense would appear to dictate that at least the minimum pool of 1500mg should be maintained, and this requires a daily intake of at least 45mg.

The Determination of Vitamin C Status

The quantity of ascorbic acid in the blood plasma gives some indication of the vitamin C status of an individual. On a daily dietary intake of 100mg, the plasma level would be about 1.2mg per 100ml, but this increases with higher intakes. After four weeks on reduced intakes of less than 10mg, plasma levels fall to 0.1mg per 100ml; at this stage, there is a moderate risk of scurvy. Levels below this indicate that the subject has a high risk of the disease.

A better measurement is the vitamin C level of the white blood cells, although this is technically more difficult. The technique involves centrifugation (spinning) of the blood, which then separates into clear plasma at the top, packed red blood cells at the bottom and a white buffy coat of white blood cells on top of the red. Careful manipulation can then remove the white blood cells. The concentration in white blood cells is usually 25 to 38mg per 100ml, which is some 20-fold the amount in plasma. When values fall below 7mg per 100ml, the subject has a high risk of scurvy.

The importance of vitamin C in the white blood cells is reflected in the fact that they are the last of the blood constituents to lose their vitamin C during periods of deprivation. The vitamin cannot be detected in plasma after 40 days deprivation, but in the white blood cells it takes 120 days for the level to drop to zero. Even so, it can take further weeks before the clinical symptoms of scurvy appear, suggesting that the body tissues that require it retain the vitamin long after it has disappeared from the blood.

Individuals can best determine their own vitamin C status with a simple test on their urine. It depends upon the fact that, after taking an oral dose of the vitamin, those replete in it will excrete most of that dose. If one is deficient there will be greater retention of the vitamin and little or none will be excreted. As vitamin C is able to decolourize certain dyes, it is a simple matter to add the dye to the urine. If the dye colour persists, there is no vitamin C present, suggesting that the oral dose has been retained. The dose can then be stepped up until vitamin C appears in the urine. There are kits available on the market, containing all the necessary ingredients for the test with full instructions.

A test more suitable for mass screening of the population has been developed by doctors in the U.K. and U.S.A. A small amount of the dye is introduced onto the tongue and the time taken for the colour to disappear is noted. Since ascorbic acid is responsible for decolourizing the dye, it follows that the more deficient in the vitamin the individual is, the longer the time taken for the colour to disappear. Any time beyond five minutes is regarded as a sign of deficiency. There is some correlation between this test and the plasma and white blood cell levels of the vitamin in the subjects studied, but the connection is not absolute.

This lingual screening test should be regarded simply as a very preliminary assessment of an individual's vitamin C status. It would separate possible subclinical deficient patients from those replete in the vitamin, but further biochemical parameters would have to be measured to confirm mild deficiency.

Body distribution of Vitamin C
Once it enters the bloodstream, vitamin C is distributed throughout the various tissues and organs of the body, but this is by no means uniform. Much of our information comes from a study carried out in 1934 in

Pittsburgh, U.S.A. by Dr Yavorsky and his colleagues, who assayed vitamin C in post-mortem tissues from individuals in various age groups. The glands are very rich in ascorbic acid with the adrenals (those producing anti-stress hormones), containing more per gram than any other organ and some 50 times richer than blood plasma. The brain and liver have low concentrations but because they are large organs the total quantity present is high.

The largest store appears to be the muscles. In a 70kg person, muscles account for 30kg of the body weight and some 600mg of ascorbic acid. This represents the main pool of the vitamin and may explain why the earliest signs of scurvy always include fatigue and lethargy. This is because ascorbic acid is concerned in the contraction mechanism of muscles, but this will be discussed later in the book.

The aqueous humour of the eye (the liquid in the front chamber of the eye that bathes the lens), contains a much higher content of vitamin C than blood plasma. In a study on rabbits, the aqueous humour was found to contain more than ten times the concentration of vitamin C than plasma and, after taking vitamin C, it increased almost three-fold. These findings, which also apply to human beings, may be related to claims by Dr M. Virno and his colleagues and also by Dr G. B. Bietti, who reported respectively in the *Eye, Ear, Nose and Throat Monthly* (1967) and the *Ophthalmological Society of Australia* (1967) that doses of 30g to 40g of vitamin C taken daily for seven months helped in the treatment of glaucoma, a condition where excessive pressure builds up in the eye.

The Urinary Excretion of Vitamin C
Under ordinary dietary intakes, the kidney zealously retains all the vitamin C present in the blood. As intake rises, blood levels increase until a concentration of 1.4mg per 100ml is achieved. Anything above this level

cannot be retained by the kidney, so the vitamin appears in the urine. The critical level above which the kidney excretes vitamin C is achieved by an intake of 140mg per day. Hence out of an oral dose of 1000mg of ascorbic acid, some 20 to 25 per cent of it is excreted in six hours in those who are not depleted of the vitamin.

These figures apply to normal healthy individuals, but excretory patterns change in certain illnesses. For example, Dr H. Vander Kamp reported in the *International Journal of Neurochemistry and Psychiatry* in 1966 that studies on longstanding chronic schizophrenic patients indicated that they needed ten times the amount of vitamin C than that of a normal individual to cause a similar pattern of excretion. Similar studies by Dr Linus Pauling (1973) on acute schizophrenic subjects confirmed that those suffering from this disease retain much more of the vitamin than control subjects.

The full significance of these findings is not yet understood, but it would appear logical that in schizophrenia there is a much greater requirement for vitamin C, so supplementation to fulfil this is a sensible measure. Although some official authorities decry taking sufficient ascorbic acid to cause excretion as wasteful, there is a positive effect of this upon the urinary system. Dr Linus Pauling, in his book *Vitamin C and the Common Cold*, suggests that ascorbic acid in high concentration in the urine protects against infection by virtue of its acidity. It may also play a part in preventing cancer of the bladder by inactivating any cancer-forming substances that may be present. An acid urine is often desirable in some conditions and this may be achieved with as small an intake as 1000mg per day.

Our Daily Needs of Vitamin C

A study carried out under the auspices of the Medical Research Council in Sheffield during 1953 showed that

20mg of ascorbic acid per day can prevent or cure overt signs of experimental scurvy in adults. This finding was confirmed by the Iowa State Penitentiary studies mentioned previously, in which techniques utilizing radioactive ascorbic acid were used. The U.K. authorities therefore suggest this amount as sufficient to prevent the signs of scurvy with an added margin of 10mg per day as a safety measure. The figure of 30mg per day is the lowest Recommended Daily Allowance (R.D.A.) amongst those countries who suggest one, as Table 1 indicates. The higher figures tend to be associated with those countries where tissue saturation is advocated.

Table 1

Recommended Daily Allowances of Vitamin C Throughout the World (mg)

	Babies	Pregnant and Lactating Women	Adults
U.K.	20	60	30
Uruguay	20	50	30
Malaysia	20	50	30
Australia	30	60	30
Norway	15	60	35
Colombia	30	50	40
East Germany	35	65	45
Italy	35	60	45
South Africa	35	80	45
Holland	30	100	50
Mexico	40	80	50
India	30	80	50
Japan	35	90	50
Czechoslovakia	30	100	60
U.S.A.	35	100	60
France	35	100	70
Philippines	30	90	75
West Germany	35	110	75
Switzerland	75	75	75
Russia	75	200	100

The wide variation of R.D.A. throughout the world

simply reflects the fact that no one is really sure how much we need for the maintenance of good health. The figures given are the minimum to prevent scurvy but what are the optimum intakes required? These could be five, ten or even fifteen-fold the R.D.A. figures, to ensure good health.

No account is taken of individual variation in requirements. When Magellan sailed the world, the privations of the crew due to scurvy were vividly recorded by crew member, Antonio Pigafetta, but it is highly significant that some sailors showed no signs of the disease and stayed perfectly healthy. Perhaps some members of the crew ate better or more wisely than others and certainly the better diets of officers probably contributed to their lower incidence of the disease. Nevertheless, there is no doubt that some individuals had an innate resistance to scurvy because their requirements were different. Experimental evidence from tests on guinea-pigs shows that some animals need 20-times more vitamin C than others to protect themselves against scurvy. Might not man also have a similar wide variation in requirements?

Another approach to determining our daily needs of vitamin C is to study how much is made by those animals that are able to synthesize it themselves. It is not unreasonable to suppose that these species will simply synthesize the amount they need, as any excess is superfluous. Studies reported in the *Journal of Biological Chemistry* (1954) and *The Annals of the New York Academy of Sciences* (1961) indicated that rats synthesize between 26 and 58mg of ascorbic acid per day, presumably because they need it. The range reflects individual variation showing, presumably that some require more than others. On the same scale, a 70kg (11 stone) human being would manufacture between 1.8g and 4.1g per day on a comparable basis.

Primates are generally recognized as the nearest animals to man in the evolutionary chain and they too have a dietary requirement for vitamin C. Primates are vegetarian, so in the wild state with ample fruit and vegetables available they would be expected to have a high intake of ascorbic acid. This is so and a gorilla's diet has been calculated by Dr G. H. Bourne and reported in the *British Journal of Nutrition* (1949) to provide 4.5g of vitamin C per day. On a similar diet an adult person would receive 2.3g of the vitamin.

Experimental monkeys need various amounts of ascorbic acid for optimum health, depending upon the particular species studied, and these quantities translate in a 70kg (11 stone) man to between 1.75 and 3.5g per day. Guinea-pigs are not primates, but they do require an extraneous source of vitamin C. They were reported by Dr M. S. Yew in *Proceedings of the National Academy of Sciences, U.S.A.* (1973) to require at least 5mg of ascorbic acid per 100g body weight per day for optimum health under ordinary circumstances, but needs increased when living under stressful conditions. On a par with these figures, the average adult person should therefore need a daily intake of at least 3.5g vitamin C.

No doubt when primitive man lived as apes, monkeys and gorillas live at present, in the wild, his intake of ascorbic acid was high because during his wanderings he would live off plants. Once he became a hunter, and thus a meat-eater, plants would have become of less importance in his diet, and his intake of vitamin C would have been reduced because meat is not a good provider of the vitamin. The human body would then adapt to lower intakes of the vitamin as generations progressed, probably by developing a more efficient mechanism of conserving it.

The fact remains, however, that even the highest R.D.A. in Table 1 is some twenty-five times less than the requirements calculated from other species. The difference is that human R.D.A. are based on the minimum amount to prevent the gross deficiency disease, scurvy, while the higher figures relate to the quantity needed for optimum health. We may know the signs and symptoms of severe vitamin C deficiency, but much less is certain about the accumulative effects of long term sub-optimal intakes. It would therefore appear to be a sensible measure to ensure a high intake of vitamin C daily, by eating foods known to be rich in it with perhaps supplementary forms of the vitamin to guarantee this intake.

Most people will ensure an optimal intake by taking between 250mg and 500mg. Even this may need to be increased during certain periods of life, in conditions of stress, when taking medicinal drugs and if one's life-style demands it. Under such circumstances, the individual may feel the need for at least 1000mg per day. Quantities above this may be required for certain therapeutic treatments and these will be dealt with later in the book. Those conditions which demand a higher intake, simply to keep body levels of vitamin C up, will be discussed later in the book.

CHAPTER 2

VITAMIN C IN FOOD

Nature is generous in her provision of vitamin C in the foods we eat and its distribution is widespread through-out the plant kingdom. Fresh fruits and vegetables are amongst the commoner natural sources although the quantities of the vitamin present vary amongst species and even in different samples of the same species, depending upon degree of ripeness and source. Recent studies from Israel and California have indicated that climatic conditions are more important than the soil quality in determining the vitamin C content of oranges. Trees growing in coastal areas bore fruit that invariably contained more of the vitamin than in those that grew inland, despite identical soil in both areas.

Pride of place for vitamin C content in readily available foods must go to blackcurrants, broccoli spears, kale, parsley and the red and green peppers both sweet and hot. However, even these are lower in the vitamin than the more exotic fruits like acerola cherry and camu-camu plum. Excellent sources amongst the more common vegetables are brussels sprouts, cabbage, cauliflower, chives and mustard greens.

Citrus fruits, despite their common acceptance as good providers of vitamin C, in fact rank only with tomatoes, radishes, spinach, strawberries, artichokes and asparagus when viewed in quantitative terms. The great advantage of citrus fruits is that while the tough skin is intact the vitamin within tends to be stable, and this property allows transport of the fruit to be undertaken with most of the vitamin C being retained. Hence the popularity of limes, oranges and lemons as providers of vitamin C during the long voyages undertaken by the old sailing ships.

The large surface area of green leafy vegetables and the ease with which they bruise, makes the vitamin more amenable to breakdown during picking and carriage, so there should be minimal delay before eating them. Dried fruits are devoid of the vitamin and nuts virtually so.

Apples vary tremendously in their ascorbic acid content, from 5mg per 100g of unpeeled Cox's Orange Pippin to 30mg per 100g in unpeeled Sturmer Pippin. In some apples there is more of the vitamin in the peel than in the flesh, so eating the whole fruit is advantageous. Cooking apples contain more vitamin C than most eaters, even when baked.

Potatoes do not represent a particularly rich source of ascorbic acid but the relatively large amount eaten in the usual diet provides important quantities of the vitamin. They provide, on average about one third of the vitamin C intake, but in winter this increases to one half when other sources are not so freely available and the total vitamin C intake is less. Unfortunately as the potato ages, its vitamin C content declines, so intakes of the vegetable which may remain constant over the year will provide less ascorbic acid in the months immediately before arrival of the new crop. Weight-watchers who deny themselves potatoes because of their calorie content should therefore ensure that they are receiving their vitamin C from other foods.

Amongst the meats, liver is a moderate source of ascorbic acid as is other offal, but on the whole, muscle meat is poor. In the absence of plant foods, however, the small amounts of vitamin C provided by meat assumes importance in preventing the development of deficiency. History provided a classic example of this when the allied garrison of Kut was besieged during the Mesopotamian campaign of 1916. The British soldiers were forced to eat their horses when other food became scarce, and none of them suffered from gross vitamin C deficiency. The Indian troops who declined horseflesh for religious reasons attempted to survive on the dried foods available, but these were devoid of the vitamin and almost every one of them succumbed to scurvy.

Seeds do not contain vitamin C, but once germinated, synthesis of the vitamin proceeds apace and this fact has enabled people to ensure an adequate intake of this essential nutrient. During famine conditions in India, for example, grains and pulses are soaked in water, then allowed to germinate on blankets that are kept damp constantly. After some 30 hours, the shoots reach a length of an inch or so, at which stage they are eaten. In this form they provide between 9 and 15mg of vitamin C per ounce, which is sufficient to stave off scurvy.

Explorers have used similar techniques to provide themselves with vitamin C, since seeds are easily carried and can be allowed to germinate at will. Sir Francis Chichester in his epic solo voyage around the world managed to ensure his daily needs of vitamin C by growing mustard and cress in trays and eating the resulting plants regularly. Growth is fast, and with mustard and cress containing between 40 and 50mg of ascorbic acid per 100g there was no problem in preventing deficiency.

Explorers have not always been as prudent. When Jacques Cartier sailed up the St Lawrence river in 1536, he wintered with his crew on the site where Quebec now stands. The lack of vegetables and fruit combined with the staple diet of grains and dried meat soon induced scurvy, and twenty-five of them died. Fortunately, a friendly Indian then introduced them to the local preventative treatment which consisted of an infusion of the bark and needles of the locally-growing pine trees. This treatment produced a remarkable cure, which is not surprising since modern analysis has indicated that pine and spruce needles contain as much vitamin C as citrus fruits. The value of this unlikely source of vitamin C in preventing scurvy has also been known to the Swedes and Russians for centuries.

They are further examples of the way in which primitive communities throughout the world have always utilized local food sources to prevent scurvy, although perhaps in the case of infused pine needles the treatment may be regarded as within the province of herbal medicine rather than nutrition!

In this way, too, the acerola cherry, located in the islands of the West Indies, and the camu-camu plum, which is confined to the jungles of the Amazon have been eaten for centuries by the local inhabitants before the value of these fruits as the richest-known sources of vitamin C became apparent to modern science. For many years it was believed that the Eskimo's sole source of vitamin C was in the meat and fish that made up their staple diet. It is now known, however, that there are hardy plants and lichens that survive the low temperatures of their habitat, and they represent a rich source of vitamin C that has been appreciated by Eskimos for centuries.

The vitamin C content of foods as eaten is shown in Table 2. Foods not mentioned may be regarded as contributing very little to the diet, and some of the more exotic fruits not widely available are also ommited.

The Stability of Vitamin C in Stored Foods

Although vitamin C may be widely distributed in foods, it is also the most sensitive of the vitamins and is easily destroyed by storage, food refining, food processing and cooking, on both the commercial and domestic levels. Losses on simple storage are due to enzymic oxidation of the vitamin. Whenever vitamin C appears in nature it is accompanied by an enzyme, called ascorbic acid oxidase, which hastens the breakdown of the vitamin. Usually this is kept apart from the destructive enzyme in the living plant but, once picked, internal breakdown of the cells releases the enzyme which then acts upon the vitamin. This process is accelerated by bruising and handling of the fruit and vegetables, so the longer the period between harvesting and eating them the greater the loss of vitamin C.

Studies carried out on the vitamin C content of stored potatoes are shown in Table 3, along with the vitamin retained during various cooking processes.

Conventional storage after eight months will thus leave only one quarter of the vitamin C originally present. This decrease, combined with further losses on cooking, probably accounts for the occasional cases of scurvy seen in old people in Edinburgh. They usually occur in April and May when old potatoes are reaching the end of their shelf-lives, but never in the weeks following the introduction of the new crop of potatoes.

When apples are stored under ordinary domestic circumstances it is quite likely they will lose two thirds

Table 2

The Average Vitamin C Content of Foods as Eaten

Food	mg/100g	Food	mg/100g
Rich Sources			
Acerola Cherry juice	3390	Grapefruit — whole	40
Camu-camu pulp	2994	Grapefruit — canned	30
Rosehip Syrup	295	Lychees	40
Guavas	200	Loganberries	35
Guavas — canned	180	Potatoes — new	30
Blackcurrants	200	Spring greens	30
Blackcurrants — stewed	150	Mangoes	30
Parsley	150	Spring Onions	25
Kale	140	Limes	25
Horseradish	120	Radishes	25
Broccoli tops	110	Peas	25
Broccoli tops — boiled	34	Sweet Potatoes	25
Green Peppers	100	Swedes	25
Tomato *purée*	100	Turnips	25
		Melons	25
Good Sources		Pineapple	25
		Raspberries	25
Whole Brussels Sprouts	90	Bilberries	22
Brussels Sprouts — boiled	40	Blackberries	20
Chives	80	Tomatoes	20
Lemons — whole	80	Runner Beans	20
Lemons — juice	50	Asparagus	20
Cauliflower	60	Lettuce	15
Cauliflower — boiled	20	Apples — cooking	15
Watercress	60	Apples — eating	12
Strawberries	60	Avocado Pears	15
Savoy cabbage	60	Quinces	15
Red cabbage	55	Sweetcorn	12
Winter cabbage	55	Bananas	10
Oranges — whole	50	Rhubarb	10
Oranges — juice	50	Onion	10
Mustard tops	50	Cod Roe	30
		Brain	23
Moderate Sources		Ox Liver	23
		Sweetbread	18
White cabbage	40	Lamb's Liver	10
Mustard and Cress	40	Heart	7
Turnip tops	40	Kidney	7
Redcurrants	40	Tongue	7
Gooseberries	40	Herring	5
		Cows Milk	1.5
		Yogurt	1.8

Table 3

The Effect of Ageing and Cooking on Vitamin C Levels of Potatoes

| | Vitamin C Content mg/100g | | |
	Raw	*Boiled & Peeled*	*Baked with Jacket*
Main crop fresh dug	30	18	24
Stored 1-3 months	20	12	16
Stored 4-5 months	15	9	12
Stored 6-7 months	10	6	8
Stored 8-9 months	8	4.8	6.4

of their ascorbic acid content after only three months. Losses are even heavier with green vegetables because the vitamin is less well protected in the relatively thin leaf and because of the large surface area they present to the air. Destruction of vitamin C starts as soon as the crop is plucked from the ground. Kale, for example, can lose 1.5 per cent of its vitamin per hour, so that one third disappears after the first day.

Although cooler temperatures may reduce the extent of the loss, storage at freezing-point or below causes damage within the cells of the leaves with subsequent accelerated breakdown. A study from Finland indicated that at a temperature of 1°C, i.e. just above freezing-point, the level of vitamin C in brussels sprouts fell from 198mg to 165mg after thirty days storage in open boxes. After a further thirty days the figure was reduced to 116mg. Relatively slight reduction of the temperature to -1°C gave similar losses to those at 1°C, but at -2.5°C the figure at the end of 60 days was 84mg of the vitamin; at -5°C, further destruction occurred to leave only 31mg at the end of 60 days. Needless to say, in Scandinavia, once brussels sprouts are harvested they are quickly transferred to storage in conditions somewhat warmer than those in which they were growing.

Fruit juices, when stored in cans or bottles, retain

most of their vitamin C content but, once air is
introduced, breakdown proceeds at a rapid pace.
Studies by Dr A. E. Bender at Queen Elizabeth College
indicated that orange drink preparations lost 30-50 per
cent of their vitamin C within eight days of opening a
sealed bottle, and as much as 90 per cent after three to
four weeks. It was calculated that 3.3mg of ascorbic
acid are destroyed by 1ml of air, so the quickest way to
destroy vitamin C in a container of fruit juice, once
opened, is to shake it vigorously. Vitamin C in apple
juice is even more unstable. Losses of 50 per cent occur
in four days with 95 per cent destroyed after only
sixteen days, even when stored at the relatively low
temperature of 5°C, which is below that of the
domestic refrigerator. Hence juices are a pleasant and
convenient way to take vitamin C, but there is little
gained by storing them for long periods once the
container is opened.

Destruction of vitamin C is accelerated by traces of
certain metals like copper and by alkaline agents such
as sodium bicarbonate (baking powder). The practice
of introducing alkali to retain the fresh green-looking
colour of vegetables is highly destructive to the vitamin
C levels and can only be condemned.

Cooking Losses of Vitamin C
The losses of vitamin C induced by cooking methods
were suspected long before modern assay methods
confirmed them. A paper in the *British Medical
Journal* in 1920 reported that, despite a good supply of
cooked vegetables, 40 out of 64 children in a Vienna
hospital developed scurvy.

This observation led to a study of the influence of
cooking on the anti-scurvy activity of cabbage and, in
the absence of a suitable chemical assay, the vitamin C
quality of the cooked vegetable was assessed by a
biological assay utilizing guinea-pigs. Simple boiling of
the cabbage for twenty minutes left only 30 per cent of

the vitamin C behind; when simmered at 75°C for sixty minutes there was only 10 per cent retained. When the same cabbage was reheated there was virtually complete loss of the vitamin. Little wonder then that scurvy soon developed in children on this diet.

Not all the vitamin C lost was destroyed, in fact most of the loss could be attributed to leaching-out of the vitamin into the cooking water. If this water had been used to prepare a gravy or sauce it is likely that deficiency symptoms would never have appeared. Later studies reported by Dr Bender in the *Importance of Vitamins to Human Health* (IV Kellogg Symposium) confirm the earlier findings, and they are reproduced in Table 4.

Table 4

Average Vitamin C Losses in Domestic Cooking

Cooking technique	Percentage of Vitamin C		
	Destroyed	Leached out	Retained
Green vegetables			
Boiling (long time, much water)	12.5	52.5	35
Boiling (short time, little water)	12.5	22.5	65
Steaming	30	5	65
Pressure cooking	25	5	70
Unsliced root vegetables			
Boiling	15	20	65
Steaming	35	5	60
Pressure cooking	45	5	50

What emerges from these observations is that, when boiling vegetables, the following tips are useful:

1. Use a minimum of water or preferably steam.
2. Use the shortest time possible.
3. Short-time, high-temperature (i.e. pressure cooking) is preferable to longer-time boiling at 100°C.

4.　Use the water in which the vegetables were cooked as another food source.

The effect of various cooking methods on the vitamin C content of potatoes is given in Table 3,

The root vegetables in this study were unsliced. Greater losses would be encountered on sliced or shredded foods because a greater surface area is presented to the boiling water with more likely losses due to destruction and leaching.

A common practice, especially where large quantities of foods are cooked, is to peel potatoes and other root vegetables and soak them overnight before cooking. Up to 60 per cent of vitamin C can be lost from potatoes in this way, but the extent of the losses varies with the method of peeling. Hand-peeling is preferable to machine-peeling, mainly because the process is less damaging. Unfortunately, in institutional cooking, mechanical peeling is the usual technique, which partly explains the lower vitamin C encountered in meals at these places.

Blanching

Vegetables have to be blanched before canning or freezing, and this applies both on the domestic scale and in industry. Blanching involves brief exposure to boiling water or steam, and is necessary to inactivate the enzymes that would otherwise have detrimental effects during storage. While industrial freezing and canning is closely controlled to give the minimum losses of vitamin C, the domestic process is not, and as much as 60 per cent of the ascorbic acid can be lost, mainly due to leaching. It is difficult in the kitchen to ensure that the whole of the vegetable reaches a temperature high enough to give efficient blanching with only a short boiling time, and losses can therefore vary. Recent studies indicated that a temperature of 85°C throughout the vegetable completely inactivated the enzymes. At 70°C, destruction of the vitamin by the enzymes reached 24 per cent of the total.

For domestic blanching, maximum retention of ascorbic acid is maintained by boiling peas for one minute, sliced beans for two minutes and brussels sprouts for three-and-a-half to seven minutes, depending upon size. The secret, to retain vitamin C after blanching, is to cool the vegetables rapidly, preferably by cold air since using cold water will lead to further losses by leaching. Commercial processes are geared to this with high pressure, cold air cooling. Water used for blanching is usually discarded with subsequent loss of the vitamin C. The liquors from canned fruit and vegetables should be utilized, however, as they contain significant quantities of the vitamin.

Frozen Foods

Once blanched, further losses of vitamin C produced by freezing are very small and what is left is stable for at least a year. Further cooking of a frozen food is usually minimal, so further decrease in vitamin content is small. This is especially so when the frozen food is introduced directly into boiling water since slow thawing will lead to further losses as vitamin C leaches into the drips. As foods to be frozen are usually picked at their peak and there is only minimal time before processing, their vitamin C content is probably higher than the so-called fresh foods that may be past their peak when harvested. A study comparing the vitamin C actually eaten when peas are cooked fresh, canned and frozen is summarized in Table 5 (see page 36). Fresh cabbage, even when cooked immediately, loses two-thirds of its vitamin C by leaching and destruction. Pasteurizing of milk causes 25 per cent of the vitamin C to be destroyed, but there is little there to start with anyway.

Microwave Cooking

This is gaining in popularity, essentially because of its extreme efficiency, particularly for rapid cooking of

Table 5

**Percentage of Available Vitamin C from Peas
at Various Stages of Processing**

	Raw State	Blanching	Sterilizing	Freezing
Fresh	100	—	—	—
Canned	100	70	45	—
Frozen	100	75	—	56

	Leached out	Thawing	As eaten
Fresh	—	—	44
Canned	18	—	6
Frozen	—	41	17

frozen foods. However, a study reported in the *Journal
of the American Dietetic Association* (1961) indicated
that when conventional cooking for various vegetables
was compared with microwave cooking, only in the
cases of cabbage, peas, green beans, frozen beans and
frozen spinach was there less vitamin C in the water

Table 6

**Percentage Retention of Vitamin C in Vegetables
Cooked by Various Methods**

		Microwave oven	Boiling	Pressure Cooking
Broccoli	solid	64	60	72
	— cooking water	23	25	6
Cabbage	solid	59	42	71
	— cooking water	31	37	10
Carrots	— solid	83	80	77
	— cooking water	15	10	13
Potatoes	solid	31	76	86
	— cooking water	13	18	5

after microwave cooking. There was no difference in the vitamin C contents of the vegetables themselves. All other vegetables showed no difference between the two methods. The results are indicated in Table 6 (see page 36).

Dehydration of Foods

The process of freeze-drying involves removing water as vapour, without the intermediate formation of liquid by applying a high vacuum at a low temperature. It therefore represents one of the best methods of preserving foods while retaining almost all the vitamins. On the other hand the more widely practised hot air drying of vegetables causes widespread destruction of the vitamin C, with minimum losses put at about 15 per cent. Drying of milk causes losses similar to those due to pasteurization, but the spray-drying technique is usually superior to roller-drying in this respect.

To sum up then, it can be said that ascorbic acid is stable in foods if they are stored or cooked in acid conditions. Destruction occurs in the presence of oxygen, light, heat, alkalies and with metals such as copper.

Reducing agents such as vitamin E will not attack vitamin C because it too is a reducing agent—the two protect each other. When frying potatoes, rapid immersion into hot deep fat retains more of the vitamin than slowly frying the food in a shallow pan.

CHAPTER 3

WHEN WE MAY NEED MORE

Marginal deficiency of vitamin C, usually associated with lowered levels in the blood plasma or white blood cells, has often been encountered in studies of certain sectors of the population. There are those who are apparently healthy but because of age, pregnancy and partaking of social (or perhaps anti-social?) habits like smoking and drinking may be at risk of deficiency. Another group comprises those on regular treatment with medicinal drugs, amongst whom must be counted females taking the contraceptive pill.

There are a number of diseases and post-operative states, where those suffering from them appear to be at risk from vitamin C deficiency. This results usually from a combination of poor diet and particular medical treatments. The significance of the needs for the vitamin in these conditions is not always apparent but what is without doubt is that during conditions of stress, ascorbic acid requirements increase.

Stress Conditions

Dr James Lind, in 1753, was the first to report that scurvy was more liable to break out in ships where the crews were exposed to the stresses induced by cold and damp working conditions, rough seas with the threat of sinking, and fatigue and debilitation by other diseases. The adrenal glands determine the body's ability to withstand stress and it is believed that this ability is mediated through the production of corticosteroid hormones by these glands. It has been mentioned that the adrenals are particularly rich in ascorbic acid under natural conditions, but once fatigued they are rapidly depleted of the vitamin.

A similar depletion of ascorbic acid has been observed in those subjected to the stresses of haemorrhage and burns. When guinea-pigs develop scurvy the corticosteroid content of the adrenals is markedly diminished. Some of the effects of scurvy can be partially counteracted with natural corticosteroid hormones. Hence it is attractive to theorize that vitamin C is needed to promote the production of those hormones required to combat stress. It is not quite as simple as this since even when the adrenals are depleted of vitamin C, they are still able to synthesize hormones. These observations can be explained by postulating a mechanism whereby ascorbic acid improves the utilization of corticosteroid hormones and prolongs their action by delaying their excretion and inactivation.

A more recent demonstration of the effects of stress upon the vitamin C status of the body and indeed of the other vitamins, has also been provided by the experiences of the early astronauts. Although the dietary requirements of these people had been carefully worked out and the necessary vitamins and minerals were incorporated into their prepacked meals, their body levels of vitamins including vitamin C were low on return to earth. No one had allowed for the fact that these people were to be subjected to physical and mental stress of an order much higher than they would be on earth. This lack of forethought was reflected in their body vitamin status. The diets of later astronauts were adjusted to take care of the increased vitamin requirements in stress, and there has been no further indication of lowered body levels.

Not many of us will experience space flight to the same extent as the astronauts, but the stresses and strains of everyday living can deplete us of vitamin C and the members of the B complex. A good diet, and in some cases supplementation with vitamins can help in providing the extra requirements of these nutrients.

Medicinal Drugs

Aspirin

Two of the most commonly used drugs today are aspirin and the components of the contraceptive pill. Not only are they widely used, but they may be taken for prolonged periods, so their effect upon the vitamin status of the individual is very important. Aspirin or acetylsalicylic acid has been known since 1936 to interfere with vitamin C utilization. The drug was found to increase the urinary excretion of the vitamin in children. For instance taking two aspirin tablets (600mg of acetylsalicylic acid) by healthy subjects every six hours resulted in 100 per cent increase in the 24-hour urinary excretion of ascorbic acid. The daily intake of 2.4g taken in a dosage regime such as this, is not unusual when the drug is taken for chronic conditions like arthritis.

Perhaps it is not surprising therefore, that a constant feature in these patients is reduced levels of vitamin C in the white blood cells. These observations have led to the suggestion of supplementary vitamin C for patients receiving this therapy. Studies reported in the *Lancet* in 1973 concluded that between 200 and 300mg of vitamin C should be taken for every aspirin tablet swallowed.

Taking vitamin C with aspirin has other benefits apart from replacing the vitamin lost due to the action of the drug.

Ascorbic acid improves the efficacy of aspirin by increasing its absorption. This in turn leads to earlier pain relief, slower excretion and longer duration of effect. The side-effects of aspirin taken alone include gastric discomfort, blood loss, sedation and of course reduced vitamin C status. Extra vitamin C taken at the same time reduce all of these. A study reported in the *Lancet* in 1968 indicated that aspirin is more likely to cause gastric bleeding when ascorbic acid levels in the individual are low.

The conditions for which aspirin is taken, including the common cold, influenza, inflammatory diseases like rheumatoid arthritis and degenerative diseases like osteoarthritis, themselves create a greater requirement for ascorbic acid. Treating these diseases with aspirin will therefore exacerbate the deficiency of the vitamin. It would seem then to be a sensible precaution, to preserve a high level of ascorbic acid within the body, by supplementation of what is an excellent drug with the vitamin it is affecting.

The Contraceptive Pill (O.C.)

The influence of the components of the contraceptive pill, notably the oestrogenic one, on the vitamin C status of women who are taking it, has been researched by the Australian team of Drs M. H. and Maxine Briggs. They reported in the *Medical Journal of Australia* in 1975 that there was ample evidence of tissue unsaturation of ascorbic acid in O.C.-treated women. The urinary excretion of the vitamin was less in these women than that in similarly matched females who did not use this form of contraception, even though both groups had the same intake. As blood levels were also lower, it is reasonable to suppose that the rate of utilization of ascorbic acid is greater in the presence of the synthetic oestrogens and or progestogens present in the contraceptive preparation. At the same time, it is much more difficult to increase the blood level of ascorbic acid in these females. Saturation of the white blood cells, which is considered to be a desirable state to aim at in any individual, was only achieved by giving those on the 'Pill' 500mg vitamin C per day. The women who were not taking the 'Pill' needed only 50mg of the vitamin per day to reach the same level of white blood cell saturation.

Similar results were reported by Professor Victor Wynn in the *Lancet* (1975) in a comprehensive review of the effect of oral contraceptives on vitamin levels in general. These studies on women only confirmed

earlier investigations on guinea-pigs who were given
the components of the contraceptive pill. The treated
animals showed reduced levels of ascorbic acid in their
livers, blood, blood vessels, and significantly, their
adrenal glands. The same animals had consistently
increased blood levels of a specific protein called
caeruloplasmin which is the carrier of the mineral
copper in the blood. This protein in turn tends to cause
excessive breakdown of vitamin C. The oestrogenic
component used in the contraceptive pill is well known
to cause a similar increase of this protein in the blood of
women taking it, so there could be a similar
mechanism contributing to the increased utilization
and hence destruction of the vitamin.

The blood levels of vitamin C of women on the 'Pill'
are consistently some 30 to 40 per cent lower than those
who are not. It is therefore a wise precaution for these
females to ensure a daily intake of at least 500mg of
ascorbic acid per day. This is not impossible to obtain
from the food alone as the figures in Table 2 show.
Similar considerations apply to women being treated
with hormone replacement therapy.

It is pertinent to consider that in modern society a
female could be taking the contraceptive pill for a
period of 35 years without a break. A half-lifetime of
reduced vitamin C status must have some effect on the
health of that woman, both during and after her child-
bearing years.

Other Medicinal Drugs
Administration of the antibiotics known as tetracyclines has been shown to lower the level of ascorbic
acid in white blood cells and blood plasma in studies
carried out in India (1968) and Britain (1972). Urinary
excretion of the vitamin increases because the
antibiotic appears to prevent the normal conservation
of ascorbic acid by the kidney. The lowered white
blood cells level results in a reduced ability to resist

infection (see Chapter 4). Hence patients such as chronic bronchitics who are treated with tetracyclines for prolonged periods are at risk of both an impaired vitamin C status and weakened natural defence mechanisms.

Barbiturates, which fortunately are now giving way to safer drugs may also affect the vitamin C status of the body in much the same way that aspirin does. Corticosteroids which are used for a wide variety of illnesses can induce an illness resembling scurvy, according to a report in the *Postgraduate Medical Journal* of 1972. Minor skin haemorrhages can occur in those on long-term treatment with these drugs, but the condition can be reversed by taking supplemental vitamin C at a level of 200mg per day.

The Effect of Smoking Tobacco

There is now ample medical evidence on the destructive influence of tobacco smoke on vitamin C levels in the body. The earliest reports were from the studies of Drs L. H. Strauss and P. Scheer of the University of Cologne, who found in 1939 that smoking tobacco produced a constant and marked reduction in the urinary excretion of vitamin C. They concluded that this was due to destruction of the vitamin by the constituents of smoke. Their conclusion was confirmed later in 1952 when more sensitive methods of assay indicated an actual lowering of blood ascorbic acid in smokers. The extent of reduction was a significant 25 to 30 per cent, which was induced both by tobacco smoke and by pure nicotine.

Dr Venulet studied non-smokers who volunteered to inhale the smoke from six to eight cigarettes daily and noted that blood ascorbic acid levels were already being reduced by the third day. When they stopped smoking, normal blood levels were restored within five days. The milk of lactating mothers who smoke contains much less vitamin C than that of comparable non-smoking women. Both studies were indicative of the destructive effect of tobacco smoke on the vitamin and they culminated in the most comprehensive trial, reported in 1975.

Dr O. Pelletier carried out the study under the auspices of the Canadian Government's Health Protection Branch. Smokers and non-smokers in the twenty to sixty-four years age group were studied over a two year period. A total of 812 male and 1562 female non-smokers were compared with 1243 male and 1092 female smokers with respect to dietary intake and blood levels of ascorbic acid. The results demonstrated conclusively that cigarette smokers with dietary ascorbic acid intakes comparable to those of non-smokers had consistently lower blood levels of vitamin C. There was a 40 per cent reduction in blood ascorbic acid in those who smoked twenty or more cigarettes daily. Amongst those of the same sex, age and dietary vitamin C intake, blood levels of the vitamin amongst smokers were consistently 30 per cent lower than non-smokers. Males in the forty to sixty-four years old age group who smoked, had a staggering 50 per cent lower blood vitamin C level than non-smoking females in the same age group.

How does tobacco smoke affect body vitamin C status? In the study from Canada it was apparent that the vitamin in the diet was less available to smokers, since blood levels of smokers, measured immediately after intake of food, did not equal those of non-smokers. This observation confirmed earlier studies on guinea-pigs where tobacco smoke or nicotine was proved to delay the absorption of vitamin C and actually reduced it.

There are of course many toxic compounds present in tobacco smoke but the main constituents are nicotine, acetaldehyde and carbon monoxide. Experimental evidence by Dr A. C. Nihon, published in 1969, indicated that vitamin C has an antidotal effect against nicotine and acetaldehyde, although it is more effective with the addition of glucose, vitamin B_1 and an amino acid called L-cysteine. In addition to preventing the uptake of vitamin C from the food, these constituents of smoke also destroy the vitamin in the bloodstream and elsewhere. The lungs present a vast surface area which is necessary for the rapid exchange of oxygen and carbon dioxide in the process of respiration. The same surface area allows a very efficient uptake of the toxic components of tobacco smoke when these are inhaled. Little wonder then that researchers have found that smokers should have at least double the intake of vitamin C as non-smokers to maintain the same blood levels.

Dr W. J. MacCormack, writing in *Archives of Paediatrics* has gone further, and attempted to quantify the extra ascorbic acid required by a smoker. He suggests that each cigarette destroys 25mg of vitamin C, so anyone who smokes can insure themselves against deficiency by taking the appropriate amount.

Non-smokers need not feel complacent. Recent studies by Dr E. Cheraskin (Pankey Symposium 1981) have shown that non-smokers with spouses who smoke inhale tobacco smoke passively in sufficient quantity to cause concern. By measuring the nicotine in the blood and urine of these people, Dr Cheraskin has concluded that there is sufficient present to adversely affect vitamin C status. Blood estimations of vitamin C confirmed that they too were low in these non-smokers. It could also be significant that non-smokers married to smokers have 80 per cent of their chances of developing lung cancer.

The Effect of Alcohol
When alcohol is drunk it is very efficiently and quickly absorbed via the stomach and small intestine. Once in the bloodstream, it is transferred to the liver where

body mechanisms convert it to carbon dioxide and water, producing a lot of calories in the process. The process is a slow one, so alcohol is retained in the blood for some hours until the liver can completely detoxify it. Unfortunately only five per cent of ingested alcohol is disposed of as such, via the excretory and repiratory mechanisms of the body. The rest is converted to the poison acetaldehyde, which you may recall is also present in tobacco smoke. Under normal circumstances, acetaldehyde is further transposed, via a series of enzymic reactions to the end products carbon dioxide and water. However, the efficieny of this conversion depends upon the health of the liver and the availability of adequate vitamins and minerals.

Between them, alcohol and acetaldehyde can affect vitamins in a number of ways: (1) by preventing their absorption; (2) by inhibiting their uptake by the liver; (3) by interfering with their activation by liver cells; (4) by causing excessive excretion and (5) by simple destruction. All vitamins are affected to a certain degree, but ascorbic acid is amongst those to suffer most. It is tragic that the very vitamins and minerals needed to detoxify alcohol effectively, are those that are influenced to the highest degree by this substance and its products.

Dr Herbert Sprince and his group at the Veterans Hospital, Pennsylvania, U.S.A. have studied the toxic effects of acetaldehyde in experimental rats. They concluded that ascorbic acid is the best single detoxifying agent to prevent death when lethal amounts of acetaldehyde were given to the animals. It also helped, but less efficiently, against anaesthesia induced by lower levels of the poison. Extending these observations to man, the group point out that chronic drinkers are known to have depressed levels of vitamin C in their blood and tissues. It seems as though the lower the level of the vitamin the worse the adverse symptoms of drinking. Obviously, the higher the alcohol intake, the more vitamin C is needed to overcome its effects. Dr Sprince considers that even a moderate drinker who drinks on a regular basis should be aiming at an ascorbic acid intake of at least one gram per day.

Consistently low levels of vitamin C have been linked with heart problems, atherosclerosis, cancer, deep vein thrombosis and cirrhosis of the liver—all conditions associated with excessive drinking and smoking. We shall see later in the book, how vitamin C functions and so relates to a possible explanation of the way in which these conditions may develop. However, it may be highly significant that one of the standard emergency treatments for alcoholics admitted to a hospital in a coma is intravenous infusion with vitamin C, sometimes accompanied by other vitamins.

At the lower end of the scale, it is likely that even the moderate social drinker will benefit from an increased intake of vitamin C. It will not enable him or her to drink more without suffering the adverse effect of excessive drink. What it will do however, is to insure against the reduced vitamin C status induced by alcohol. In this way, at least one factor that may be involved in the ultimate consequences of regular drinking, that of vitamin C deficiency, will be eliminated.

The Elderly
Many surveys have been carried out to determine how vitamin C reserves vary amongst different sectors of the population. What has emerged is that a number of factors contribute to mild deficiency, among which are dietary intake, social class, season, age and the place of habitation (home, hospital, institutions etc.). Dietary intake can be decreased by poor selection of food and destructive methods of cooking and these are dealt with in Chapter 2. The lower social groups, as measured by income, also show consistently low body reserves of vitamin C. Those with higher incomes tend

to eat more C-rich foods, resulting in higher body reserves.

The seasons of the year also determine the vitamin C status of the population as a whole. This is at its lowest ebb in April and May with its peak in August and September. These variations reflect the different diets eaten during these periods because of the greater availability of new potatoes, fresh fruit and vegetables towards the latter months.

As a general rule vitamin C reserves in the body decrease as age increases. Hence, the elderly must be regarded as the largest single group of the population most prone to mild deficiency of ascorbic acid. In this group men usually have lower levels of the vitamin than women. Whether this is because of higher requirements as some have claimed, or whether they simply reflect a lower intake is not certain.

One factor that does contribute to lower vitamin C levels in the elderly, appears to be an inefficient absorption mechanism. In one study, females between the ages of sixty-five and eighty-four years had perfectly adequate food intakes of the vitamin, but their white blood cell levels were low, indicating that they were apparently unable to assimilate it. These women lived at home, pursuing active lives on wholesome diets. They represent the upper strata of their group. How then do the less fortunate elderly people who are housebound or living in institutions fare?

The answer is provided by comprehensive studies, carried out by Dr A. N. Exton-Smith and others in 1972. In housebound old people, the intakes and body levels of vitamin C were as much as 31 per cent below the accepted levels. However, elderly patients in institutions and long-stay hospitals give the most cause for concern. Their intake of ascorbic acid is low, due essentially to the poor level of the vitamin in mass-produced hospital diets. Their white blood cell concentration of vitamin C falls well below the levels of those found in subjects of comparable age who are living at home. To restore the vitamin C reserves of these in-patients to normal, requires a daily intake of some 5 to 30 times the recommended minimum intake (30mg in the U.K.).

These people showed no abject signs of scurvy, so how could these low body reserves of the vitamin affect their health? In the recent Kellogg Nutrition Symposium (1978), Dr Exton-Smith drew attention to the mental symptoms that can accompany mild ascorbic acid deficiency. They include depression and personality changes. Also many of the non-specific, vague minor illnesses and irritations can be associated with low levels of vitamin C in the aged. These signs and symptoms appear long before the more serious manifestations of scurvy.

The effect of supplementary vitamin C on these conditions in old people was reported by Dr C. J. Schorah and his colleagues from The University of Leeds in the *Lancet* (1979). All the subjects were long-stay patients aged fifty-nine to ninety-seven years from two local geriatric hospitals. Their blood plasma and white blood cell ascorbic acid levels were low compared to those in healthy controls who were blood donors. Each patient was given either 1g of vitamin C in a fruit-flavoured drink daily, or a placebo drink containing no vitamin C, for a total of 28 days. There were significant differences between the two groups. Those on vitamin C were found to have normal blood plasma levels but surprisingly, even after dosage of 1g per day the white blood cell levels were still low, although increased on the starting figure. No dramatic clinical improvement was expected in such a short time interval, but instead, the placebo group tended to deteriorate during the trial. What did happen though, was that there were significantly more clinical improvements and weight gains in those treated with the vitamin, than in the placebo groups. There was no doubt that extra vitamin C made these people feel better both physically and mentally.

A similar study on young patients who had been in hospitals or institutions for at least six months gave similar results. These, too, had low blood vitamin C levels at the start of the trial and the supplementary vitamin had a distinct tonic effect. The sad conclusion is that all patients of any group who spend long periods in institutions are at risk in their vitamin C reserves, presumably brought on by poor dietary intake.

Athletes

In view of what is known about the increased requirements of ascorbic acid during periods of stress, it would appear to be logical that athletes aim for an increased intake. They are under physical stress during their strenuous training routines and in the actual event, but there is also considerable mental stress because of the very competitive nature of their sport.

Over and above this aspect of vitamin requirements, however, is the question whether increased ascorbic acid intake can actually improve physical performance. There are as many trials suggesting that vitamin C is beneficial as there are those concluding that it is not so; the question of supplementation is still controversial. What these trials measured were changes in the respiratory and heart and blood flow functions of the body. A more recent study, reported in the *Journal of the New York Academy of Sciences* (1975), examined the possible influences of ascorbic acid intake on human muscle metabolism in a standard exercise test.

Thirteen athletes had their performance assessed on an exercise bicycle over a period of 14 days. They were then given 1g ascorbic acid per day over the next fortnight and their performance on the bicycle assessed again. There were no significant differences

on the exercise tolerance of these athletes induced by
vitamin C. Where there was a distinct improvement
was in the heart beat. When taking vitamin C the heart
beat was a siginificant eight to nine beats per minute
lower, and this persisted during the increase, from
around 90 beats at low energy expenditure to the peak
170 beats per minute. In any athlete, a lower beat rate
is usually interpreted as a sign of a better work capacity
and a more economic heart function during exercise.
In this respect, vitamin C was undoubtedly beneficial.
Further study indicated that the improvement in heart
beat appeared to be related to an increased synthesis of
the hormones, adrenaline and nor-adrenaline. These
compounds improve the volume of blood pumped at
each beat, so enabling the heart to distribute the same
output of blood, but at a lower frequency of beat.

Free fatty acids represent the major fuel required for
muscle metabolism and hence contraction. When
these athletes were dosed with vitamin C, the blood
plasma fatty acids increased significantly over those
measured during the time of placebo administration.
The greater availability of free fatty acids thus presents
the working muscle with extra fuel and preserves the
energy reserve present as muscle glycogen. In this way,
vitamin C is exhibiting a beneficial effect, especially in
long-lasting exercise. Blood glucose uptake by the
muscles is hardly affected by vitamin C, so its main
action appears to be mediated through free fatty acid
utilization.

Athletes, however, should beware of taking too
much ascorbic acid. Other studies have shown that
very high intakes of the vitamin increase oxygen utilization by working muscles. This in turn upsets the
equilibrium between oxygen transport and usage since
it can lead to a deficit in the oxygen supplied. Under
such circumstances, the athletic performance must
decrease.

CHAPTER 4
WHAT VITAMIN C DOES

Clues as to how a vitamin functions, are often given by a study of what happens when an animal or person is deprived of that vitamin. Gross deficiency of vitamin C leads to the disease scurvy, so it is pertinent at this stage to describe the signs and symptoms of that particular scourge.

The early stages of ascorbic acid deficiency in the guinea-pig and in man are common to both. They usually start with fatigue leading to tiredness on exertion and a disinclination to exercise. In the guinea-pig, there is atrophy or wasting of the muscles of the feet. Adult people also feel listless and feeble and complain of weakness, irritability, pains in the muscles and joints and loss of weight.

These symptoms of course are not confined to ascorbic acid deficiency but it is possible for them to persist for many weeks before the clearer-cut signs of scurvy manifest themselves. These appear as bleeding gums, gingivitis (inflammation of the gums) and loosening of the teeth. That part of the gum between the teeth usually swells to almost conceal the teeth. In appearance these areas are livid in colour and may bleed even on the slightest touch. The gums in this condition are very prone to infection and this in turn often causes production of a foul odour from the mouth. Babies who do not have teeth and older people who have lost them do not show these changes so that such early warning signs of scurvy may be missed.

The next stage is the appearance of minute haemor-rhages under the skin, known as petechiae, and these are first obvious on the lower thighs just above the knees where they occur around individual hairs. Eventually similar subcutaneous bleeding, due to the rupture of capillaries appears on the buttocks, abdomen, legs and arms. As greater areas become affected, large spontaneous bruises may arise anywhere on the skin particularly where slight pressure has been applied. The legs are particularly affected and these blotches are usually accompanied by pain in the thigh or calf. One of the less obvious signs of vitamin C deficiency is osteoporosis.

A study of Bantu middle-aged men in Johannesburg by Dr Harry Seftel, showed that alcoholism combined with a low ascorbic acid intake in the diet induced scurvy and osteoporosis (indicated by X-ray). In Britain it is also believed that low body levels of the vitamin may contribute to the loss of minerals from the skeleton, leading to osteoporosis.

Diagnosis of scurvy in infants is more difficult. In the absence of teeth, the gum changes are not seen and the earliest sign of scurvy is subcutaneous bleeding. This occurs first in the long bones of the limbs and gives rise to intense pain, especially on movement. Deficiency in an infant may first be noted when it cries on being handled and shows extreme tenderness of the extremities. Other symptoms which may be present at any age include haemorrhages in the white of the eye, drying up of the saliva and tears, oedema (swelling) of the lower limbs, anaemia and psychological disturbances including depression. All of the changes induced by vitamin C deficiency are reversed completely once ascorbic acid has been administered.

Helps Muscles Function

A survey of the historical descriptions of scurvy indicates that the common factor in the early signs of the disease is the appearance of muscle fatigue. Eugalems (1658) described tiredness, fatigue and an aversion to exercise as observations in scorbutic people. Spontaneous debility was noted by Lister (1696) and Sydenham (1742). Anson studied scurvy victims for four years (1740-1744) and noted extensive lassitude of the body, especially after exercise however light. Lind, in his classical studies of scurvy in 1753, mentioned listlessness, lassitude with much fatigue as common to all his subjects. Budd (1840) observed great languor and despondency with aversion to every kind of exercise in those suffering from scurvy, who were also found to become readily fatigued. Shapster (1847) studied scorbutic patients in Exeter and reported the first stage of scurvy was characterized by debility, weakness, listlessness and an aversion to exertion.

In 1936, Van Eekelen observed volunteers on a vitamin C-free diet and found that only after 84 days did fatigue and irritability appear. A similar time lapse (three months) was noted by Drs Crandon, Lund and Dill (1940) before fatigue was apparent in their volunteers, although six to eight weeks later, overt deficiency signs of scurvy appeared. Similarly, the intrepid inmates of Iowa State Prison who volunteered to be deprived of vitamin C in Dr R. E. Hodges classic studies, complained of muscle fatigue after only 84 to 97 days on their deficient diet.

The reason for all these observations is that the contraction of muscle requires the presence of the muscle component carnitine and lack of this leads to fatigue. In guinea-pigs deprived of vitamin C, muscle carnitine decreases as the deficiency gets worse. When two groups of animals were fed diets deficient in ascorbic acid, giving carnitine to one group increased their muscular activity when compared to the other. Hence, supplying the essential ingredient for muscle contraction lessened the need for vitamin C in these experiments. Confirmation of these observations has come from studies on old people who are on poor diets and complain of fatigue. They invariably have low blood levels of carnitine which are improved by vitamin C supplementation.

The association between carnitine and vitamin C is

simple. Although we obtain carnitine from the meats
in our diets, most of it is synthesized by the body from
the essential amino acid lysine. This synthesis is
absolutely dependent on vitamin C. Since they eat no
meat, vegetarians rely completely upon lysine as the
precursor of carnitine in their muscles, so their intake
of vitamin C must be adequate for this conversion.
Usually of course, vegetarians are likely to have a
higher intake of ascorbic acid than meat-eaters, so lack
of carnitine in the diet is well compensated for. It is of
interest that the old name for carnitine is vitamin B_T,
because before its body synthesis from lysine was
discovered, it was regarded as an essential food factor.

Why is carnitine so important in muscle contraction? The reason is that carnitine is essential to transport fatty acids within the muscle cells. Once inside the
energy-producing parts of the cell, known as mito-
chondria, these fatty acids are converted into energy.
The muscle is able to utilize this energy in its contraction. Heart muscle also needs fatty acids for energy,
and carnitine is the essential carrier that ensures this
vital organ gets the energy it needs in order to beat
Heart failure is often a cause of death in those suffering
from scurvy and the reason can be traced to a deficiency of carnitine, brought on by lack of vitamin C.

Helps Iron Absorption

Iron in nature exists in two forms known as ferrous and
ferric. It is generally believed that iron is absorbed
from the food we eat, only in the ferrous form. Hence
any iron that we eat in the ferric form must be reduced
to ferrous iron, and as ascorbic acid is a strong
reducing-agent and is present in the diet, it is likely
that it helps in this manner. This function of vitamin C
however, only applies to the iron available from non-
meat food sources.

In the diet, iron exists as haem-iron, present only in
meats and as non-haem-iron, the form in which it

occurs in cereals, vegetables, fruits etc., i.e. non-animal foods. In Western countries, the meat-eating population obtains only ten per cent of its dietary iron in the haem form, with the remaining 90 per cent available as the non-haem type. Vegetarians and the vast populations of the developing countries receive all their dietary iron in the non-haem form. Hence, in any individual non-haem iron represents his or her main source of this essential mineral, so the efficiency of its absorption is of paramount importance.

Dr L. Hallberg of the Department of Medicine, University of Göteborg in Sweden has studied this problem by measuring the uptake of radioactive iron from non-haem sources in human volunteers. His results were reported at a vitamin C symposium held at the University of Warwick in 1981. Various kinds of food were labelled with the radioactive non-haem iron and the effect of adding vitamin C was observed. Whenever vitamin C was added, it was either sprinkled onto the food as a powder or taken as a tablet with the food, or taken as a food item. The results are shown in Table 7 (see page 57).

The results indicated that vitamin C is effective in increasing non-haem-iron absorption, whether added separately or as a vitamin C rich food. The vitamin has no effect upon the absorption of haem-iron, which shows that the mechanism for absorbing the two types of iron must be different. In the continental breakfast, the beneficial effect of the ascorbic acid was partly neutralized by the tea. This is because tea contains tannin which can precipitate and hence immobilize the iron, making it unavailable for absorption. Coffee has no tannin so the availability of the iron was not affected by it.

Iron salts when taken as supplements are like non-haem-iron, so vitamin C is essential for effective absorption. Amino acid chelated iron is comparable to haem-iron in its structure, also it is not dependent on the vitamin. This explains the superior absorption of

Table 7

The Effect of Vitamin C on Iron Absorption

Meal Eaten	Vitamin C added	Iron absorbed with C (mg)	Iron absorbed without C (mg)
Pizza	50mg	0.57	0.19
Hamburger	50mg	0.55	0.32
Continental breakfast/ coffee	50mg	0.40	0.16
Continental breakfast/ tea	50mg	0.21	0.07
Vegetable salad	45mg	0.48	0.26
Cooked cauliflower	45mg	1.05	0.44
Vegetables with low C content	—	—	0.13
Vegetables with low C content + cauliflower	—	0.32	—
Vegetables with low C content + meat	—	—	0.25
Vegetables with low C content + fish	—	—	0.44
Vegetables with high C content	—	0.98	—
Vegetables with high C content + meat	—	1.42	—

amino acid chelated iron compared to that of iron salts, even in the presence of ascorbic acid.

What emerges from the study is the important finding that intakes of vitamin C, lower than 50mg per meal had no effect upon the absorption of non-haem-iron. This makes nonsense of the suggested daily intake of 30mg vitamin C per day (i.e. 10mg with each meal), suggested by U.K. authorities as all that is needed. Dr Hallberg concludes that the world-wide deficiency of iron might be better overcome by increasing the absorption of that in the food with added ascorbic acid, rather than by supplementary iron. This view is shared by Dr D. Derman and his co-workers from the University of the Witwatersrand and the University of Natal, who reported similar results from their studies on South African housewives of Indian descent. These findings emphasize the importance of eating vitamin C with meals, even when taken as a supplement, if one is to gain most benefit.

Forms Collagen

Collagen is a fibrous protein that has a supportive and protective role in the connective tissue of the skin, joints and vital organs of the body. Partial breakdown of collagen produces gelatin, a protein much used in the food industry. When the skin or body tissues are wounded either by accident or by surgery, the rate at which healing takes place depends on the ability of the body to produce new collagen. This production is under the control of vitamin C.

Collagen is, like all proteins, a complex structure made up of various amino acids present in varying proportions. About one quarter of these amino acids are provided by glycine, the simplest amino acid and between them, proline and hydroxyproline account for a further third of the constituent amino acids. Hydroxyproline is unique because it is not found in any other protein, but its role in maintaining the structure of collagen is crucial. In its absence, collagen can be formed, but the protein is weak because it lacks the cross links provided by hydroxyproline, and so it breaks easily. The only way that hydroxyproline can be made by the body is by conversion from proline, an amino acid provided by the food. This conversion is absolutely dependent upon adequate levels of vitamin C. Hence, it is easy to understand the fundamental role that the vitamin has in the production of hydroxyproline, which in turn contributes to the strength of collagen.

Bone also has a high content of collagen, so its rate of mending after fracture is also dependent on vitamin C. A classic example of the role of vitamin C in healing tissues and bones is provided by R. Walter in his book describing *Lord Anson's Voyage Round the World 1740-1744*. A man on the ship had been wounded fifty years before and his wounds had healed satisfactorily. He was one of the unfortunates who contracted scurvy during the voyage and, amazingly, all the scars and the broken bone from his previous wounding opened up again as if they had never healed. Collagen is not a static protein and is continually being degraded and built up within the tissues. With the lack of vitamin C, synthesis of the stronger collagen was not able to take place and the weaker areas gave way first. It has long been known that delayed wound healing is a feature of scurvy. Vitamin C must therefore be regarded as a key factor in the efficiency of wound healing.

It has been amply demonstrated that a surgical operation causes a fall in the levels of blood plasma and white blood cell ascorbic acid. The vitamin is not excreted, so presumably there is a redistribution amongst the body tissues. It would be attractive to suggest that it concentrates at the wound, but this is not yet definitely proved. What is established is that lack of vitamin C in an individual delays wound healing. With the knowledge that many sectors of the population have low intakes of vitamin C, and of the notoriously low level of the vitamin in many hospital diets, it would be fortuitous for anyone contemplating surgery to ensure they have adequate levels in their bodies. Many surgical units now supplement their patients with ascorbic acid before the actual operation.

A constant problem with long-term bed-ridden patients is their tendency to develop bed-sores known by the medical term, decubitus ulcers. They are formed by a combination of unrelieved pressure at certain parts of the body (usually bony prominences like the hip), and poor nutrition.

A double-blind trial carried out at Manchester Royal Infirmary and reported in the *Lancet* (1974), confirmed the role of poor nutrition in slowing down the healing of these ulcers. Ten surgical patients were given 500mg of ascorbic acid daily and ten others were given a harmless placebo tablet, identical in appearance to that containing vitamin C. All twenty patients had similar blood levels of the vitamin before the trial, but within one month, those of the group receiving ascorbic acid were three times higher than the group receiving placebo. With the higher levels of vitamin C came a big improvement in the healing rate of the bedsores. The reduction in numbers of those of the treated patients was twice that of the untreated. Most of those receiving vitamin C had ulcers that healed completely in less than a month; the placebo group took three to four months. The basic process in healing is the production of collagen leading to new tissues, and this is determined by the presence of adequate vitamin C. Perhaps there is logic after all in the practice of taking fresh fruit into hospital patients!

Resists Infection

Another aspect of scurvy is the ease with which the victim succumbs to infections, suggesting that lack of ascorbic acid weakens the individual's resistance to disease. We have already seen that one of the most important sites of vitamin C concentration is in the white cells of the blood. These we know are intimately concerned with resisting infection, and modern research has now suggested how vitamin C may function in these cells.

White blood cells are of two main types, the phagocytes or polymorphonuclear cells and the lymphocytes. What happens when a microorganism invades the body is that it becomes attached to a specific antibody. The combination then activates a special substance present in blood plasma known as complement, which causes the phagocytes to approach the combination and engulf it. The efficiency of phagocytes to carry out this operation depends upon two factors. First is the mobility of the cell to reach the invading microorganism and second is the antimicrobial action, once contact is made. Both functions are stimulated by vitamin C. It is possible to measure the mobility of phagocytes and Professor R. Anderson of the University of Pretoria in South Africa has demonstrated that patients with increased susceptibility to infection have phagocytes with low mobility. When these people are given vitamin C at the rate of 3g daily, there is a dramatic increase in the speed of reaction of the phagocytes to invading microorganisms, as well as an enhanced ability to destroy them.

The development of antibodies which are produced in response to specific microorganisms (antigens) are the responsibility of the second type of white blood cell, the lymphocytes. These also can only function effectively in the presence of ascorbic acid. At the Vitamin C Symposium held at Warwick University in 1981, Professor Anderson quoted two instances where lymphocyte function was stimulated by vitamin C.

The first condition is granulomatous disease of children, whereby the child cannot synthesize the enzymes needed to produce antibodies. Consequently, they are open to every type of infection. Giving vitamin C allowed a normal immune system to develop and they have been infection-free for two years. A second condition is allergic bronchial asthma. Ten children suffering from this disease were treated with vitamin C at a rate of 1g per day. Six of them had lymphocytes which were deficient in inducing an immune response, but after ascorbic acid treatment the system became normal. Two had evidence of a low mobility of their phagocytes, which responded to the vitamin and produced normal activity. Two showed no response, suggesting that their condition could not be attributed to low vitamin C levels. This research is very recent, but it proves that ascorbic acid is needed for an efficient system against infection and could be part of the reason why the vitamin may also help against virus diseases like colds and influenza. In these reactions, vitamin C appears to be acting as a specific anti-oxidant.

Reduces High Blood Cholesterol

When guinea-pigs are deprived of vitamin C, cholesterol levels increase in the blood, and fats are deposited in the walls of blood vessels, particularly those of the heart and brain. These animals also show a greater tendency to form gallstones. Most gall-stones in any species, including man, are composed of cholesterol and they tend to form by precipitation when bile cholesterol levels increase. This is precisely what happens in the C-deficient guinea-pigs. Modern research suggests that vitamin C has an important function in controlling blood cholesterol and fat levels in human beings also.

The leading researcher in this field is Dr E. Ginter of the Institute of Human Nutrition Research, Bratislava, Czechoslovakia. He studied the relationship between vitamin C levels in the white blood cells and the concentration of cholesterol and fats in the blood of a large number of patients, both male and female. The highly significant result to emerge, was that the lower the vitamin C level in these people, the higher were the cholesterol and blood fat levels. The next stage was to determine if cholesterol and fat levels could be reduced by increasing the vitamin C intake and this is exactly what Dr Ginter found. Diabetic patients (who usually have high blood cholesterol), and others who had high blood cholesterol levels with no obvious cause were treated with 500mg vitamin C per day. The blood cholesterol levels and the total fat in the blood were reduced in all cases. This reduction was maintained while those patients were given ample vitamin C. Similar supplementation on a group of patients who did not have high cholesterol levels had no effect. In other words, ascorbic acid will reduce excessive cholesterol, but once normal levels are achieved it has no further influence.

How does vitamin C achieve cholesterol reduction? It increases the rate at which cholesterol is converted into bile acids and hence excreted. In his patients Dr Ginter found no evidence of a higher excretion of cholesterol as such, but what did increase dramatically was their excretion of bile acids. The usual route through which the body disposes of cholesterol is to convert it into bile acids in the liver, which are then deposited in the bile, carried to the intestine where they assist in fat digestion and end up excreted in the faeces. Speeding up this process neatly disposes of excess cholesterol. Drugs that decrease cholesterol usually do so by preventing its synthesis by the body. Recently however these drugs have received adverse publicity because of their serious side-effects. It looks now as though we have in vitamin C a safe, effective treatment that works in a more logical manner, by accelerating the disposal of cholesterol. Blood fats are also reduced by vitamin C, but although the mechanism is not completely worked out, the vitamin is just as effective and safe.

There may be other benefits from an intake of 500mg of ascorbic acid daily. Dr Geoffrey Taylor, formerly professor of medicine at the University of Lahore, has reported that changes in the tiny blood vessels, particularly those under the tongue, may be the warning signs of impending stroke. These changes also appear in scurvy and in mild deficiency of vitamin C. The number of deaths from strokes and coronary heart disease increase in cold weather in the winter, when the need for ascorbic acid is highest, but intake is at its lowest. Dr Constance Lesley of the Wakefield Group of Hospitals in Yorkshire is another expert who has found that vitamin C exerts a powerful protective effect on certain high risk groups of the population. It could help prevent heart attacks, strokes, deep vein thrombosis and atherosclerosis through its fat-controlling function as described by Dr Ginter.

We know that fat is only one factor in increasing the risks of these conditions. Stress, diet, smoking and alcohol also may contribute. Yet we have seen that all of these may lower the vitamin C levels of the body by poor intake or excessive destruction or increased requirements of the vitamin. Vegetarians who have a high intake of vitamin C and various other groups who, for religious or ethical reasons do not partake of the lifestyle dictated by the other factors, all have lower incidences of the diseases mentioned. Perhaps we should all look to our vitamin C intakes as one of the sensible means to reduce the chances of these blood-related diseases.

Other Functions

There are other less well-established functions that we can attribute to ascorbic acid. These include its role in converting the B vitamin, folic acid (the anti-anaemia vitamin) into its active form, folinic acid. Malfunctioning of this conversion could explain the particular type of anaemia seen in scorbutic patients.

Vitamin C appears to have a mutual protective effect on vitamin E. When vitamin E is functioning in its own protective role, it is converted to another product. Ascorbic acid ensures that this product is regenerated back to vitamin E. Similarly vitamin E has the ability to prevent vitamin C from being destroyed. Both vitamins must be regarded as the great protectors of the body.

Finally, ascorbic acid is concerned with the conversion of amino acids to substances in the brain required for normal brain and nervous function. The mental effects of scurvy have been well documented and the greater mental alertness of old people with low body levels of vitamin C after treatment with the vitamin is also well established. The hormone adrenaline is also protected by ascorbic acid.

CHAPTER 5

THERAPEUTIC BENEFITS OF VITAMIN C

The controversy over the possible benefits of ascorbic acid in preventing and treating the common cold, may be thought to be modern, but early trials in fact took place in the 1930s. The first on record is that by Dr Roger Korbsch of Oberhausen, Germany who found that 1000mg per day, taken orally, helped relieve the nasal symptoms of the common cold. He noted that an injection of 250mg or 500mg of ascorbic acid immediately cold symptoms appeared, more often than not suppressed the cold, although occasionally a second injection was needed.

These promising results led other investigators to look at the therapeutic properties of vitamin C and in 1938 Dr S. L. Ruskin carried out a larger scale trial on over 1000 patients. He reported in the *Annals of Otology, Rhinology and Laryngology* that an injection of calcium ascorbate (a neutralized form of ascorbic acid), given on the first appearance of a cold, prevented completely its development in 42 per cent of his patients. A further 48 per cent of those treated, were markedly improved, giving a credible 90 per cent response to prompt treatment with vitamin C.

It could be highly significant that both these successful trials utilized the vitamin in an injectable form, which ensured high body levels quickly. Studies carried out in later years, tended to give ascorbic acid by mouth, and it is doubtful that comparable blood and tissue levels would be achieved as quickly by this route.

The first of many controlled clinical trials where the effect of orally-administered ascorbic acid was assessed, was from Scotland in 1942 where Drs A. J. Glazebrook and S. Thomson studied 1435 students. They had the great advantage that all the students were in one institution, were all of the same age group (15 to 20 years), and were thus better controlled as far as dosing and observation was concerned. The treated group, 335 in number, were given 200mg of ascorbic acid per day for a period of six months. The control group, who numbered 1100, subsisted on a typical institution diet which provided only between 5 and 15mg of vitamin C per day.

The differences between the two groups, while not outstanding, did indicate some beneficial effect of the added vitamin. Colds and tonsillitis affected 34.5 per cent of the controls, and only 30.1 per cent of the treated students. Of those affected, most coped with their condition, but some had to be admitted to the sick bay when they showed more serious symptoms. Again, more (30.5 per cent) of the control group affected, required medical treatment than the treated one (23 per cent). The number of days this medical treatment was required was two-and-a-half for those receiving ascorbic acid, and five days for those not receiving the extra vitamin. Pneumonia and other serious respiratory diseases, developed eventually in 33 of the students on normal diets, but none of the treated group reached this stage of illness.

This trial is typical of most of the studies carried out, on the effect of vitamin C upon the common cold. It can be criticized on the grounds that the dose of the vitamin was too small, the differences between the two groups, although significant were also small, and the fact that 1100 controls were compared to only 335 treated students, when the ideal would have been equal numbers of each. The students were all male, so the study gave no indication on what would happen in females, similarly treated.

An identical dose of 200mg was given to some students (mixed male and female) at the University of Minnesota in a trial organized by Drs W. D. Cowan, H. S. Diehl and A. B. Baker, during the winter of 1939-1940. Two hundred received a 100mg tablet of ascorbic acid per day, and 200 received a harmless placebo for a period of 28 weeks. The investigators concluded that at this level, vitamin C did not have a significant effect upon the number or severity of infections of the nose, throat and chest. Dr Linus Pauling has reassessed the results of this trial and concluded that there was a small, though significant benefit endowed by vitamin C. Even the assessment of a positive response can be controversial.

The main criticism aimed at these trials was that the quantity of ascorbic acid given daily was too small. We have seen previously that theoretically this quantity should be sufficient to saturate the tissues of the body, although biological variation means that some individuals would require much more to achieve saturation. Accordingly, a carefully controlled study with the relatively large amount of 1000mg vitamin C was carried out by Dr G. Ritzel of Switzerland. All of the 279 subjects were boys of similar age (15 to 17 years) and there were two periods of study, namely five and seven days. Neither the investigators nor the boys knew whether they were taking their gram of ascorbic acid per day or a harmless placebo, so the trial was truly double-blind. The boys were examined daily by medical methods, for symptoms of colds and other infections and were also assessed on their own judgement of symptoms. There was no doubt in this trial that vitamin C at the level given was of benefit in preventing and treating colds. Of the 140 subjects receiving placebo, 31 developed colds as against 17 out of 139 of those receiving 1000mg of vitamin C. Moreover, the duration of the colds was some 29 per cent less in the treated boys than those on placebo tablets.

A similar double-blind trial involving 641 children in a Navajo boarding school gave comparable results. Dr J. L. Coulehan and his colleagues reported in the *New England Journal of Medicine* (1974), that giving 321 children 1g or 2g of ascorbic acid per day over 14 weeks reduced the average number of days with colds by 30 per cent over a similar number of children not treated. They benefited in other ways too; in total, there was 17 per cent less time off sick, involving diseases other than those of the respiratory tract.

A series of clinical trials from Toronto, Canada probably represent the best controlled and meaningful studies carried out on large numbers of subjects. All three have been reported in the *Canadian Medical Association Journal* by Dr T. W. Anderson and various colleagues. In the first, 407 subjects received 1g of ascorbic acid per day, plus 3g per day at the onset of any illness. A total of 411 subjects received a placebo, and both regimes were continued for four months. When both groups were matched on the duration of any illness, the ascorbic acid-treated subjects had 30 per cent less time confined to their houses, with 33 per cent less time off work.

The second trial involved 2349 persons in eight treatment groups, over a period of three months. Two groups received a placebo; one group was given 250mg of vitamin C daily; one group received 1g daily; one group received 2g daily; two groups were given 4g and 8g on the first day of any illness and the last group took 1g daily plus 4g on the first day of any illness. The results were disappointing in that there appeared to be only marginal and probably insignificant benefit of ascorbic acid in prevention of disease, and there was no evidence that an increased dose was any better than the lowest one of 250mg per day. There was no doubt, however, that the large therapeutic doses of 4g and 8g per day, when taken at the immediate onset of illness, did reduce the duration and extent of disability from acute infections. One of the problems pinpointed by the investigators was the difficulty of an accurate diagnosis of the common cold in such a large population.

Accordingly, the way was now open for the third Toronto trial when a smaller number of subjects, 488, were split into three groups. During the fifteen-week study, 150 people received a weekly 500mg tablet of vitamin C; 152 were given a weekly 500mg sustained release capsule and the remainder received a placebo tablet. All subjects were instructed to take an extra tablet or capsule at the onset of any illness and to repeat if necessary. All subjects were assessed for the symptoms of respiratory disease and for their mental attitude. The investigators concluded that 'subjects in both vitamin groups experienced less severe illness than subjects in the placebo group, with approximately 25 per cent fewer days spent indoors because of illness'.

Hence, these results are comparable to those of the first study. However, one important fact to emerge from this study was that there was as much protection against non-respiratory illness as against that affecting the respiratory tract. In their opinion; 'Taken in conjunction with the positive results reported by other investigators, there is now little doubt that the intake of additional vitamin C can lead to a reduced burden of "winter illness"'.

Another approach to clinical study of vitamin C and the common cold has been made by the Common Cold Research Unit in Salisbury, U.K. In one trial, volunteers were actually inoculated with one of five known viruses producing the common cold. Forty-four of these people were given 3g of vitamin C per day, the rest were given placebo. On the third day they received the virus. Some developed colds and some didn't, but there was no significant difference in the severity and duration of the colds in either group. Unfortunately, administration of the tablets was stopped three days after the onset of illness and the illness itself lasted five days longer. Hence, lack of treatment on the last two days could have prolonged the duration of the colds. It is well established that when a high intake of vitamin C is suddenly stopped the blood level of the vitamin decreases dramatically for a few days to very low levels, and therefore this measure could have contributed to a longer term of illness. Even when a cold appears to have cleared up quickly on ascorbic acid treatment, dosing at the same high level should continue for several days at least.

A second trial was a joint effort between the Common Cold Research Unit at Salisbury and North-wick Park Hospital, Harrow. It involved 753 men and 771 women, taken from various climatic, cultural and nutritional environments in the U.K. The trial was randomized and double-blind, and it was designed to assess the effect of ascorbic acid on the symptoms of a cold, rather that its preventative effect. The dose was four 1g effervescent tablets of vitamin C daily for two-and-a-half days administered as soon as the volunteers experienced the symptoms of a cold. The controls received an effervescent placebo. The results showed that colds occurred with equal frequency in volunteers on the vitamin or placebo and about 30 per cent of those studied had at least one cold. There was no evidence that cold symptoms were relieved by taking ascorbic acid, neither were there reductions of time in bed, time off work or duration of the cold.

The only significant difference in response in this trial, was related to the sex of the volunteers. Of the males in the study, fewer of those on ascorbic acid had two or more colds than those on placebo. This difference was not significant in the females. The objections to this trial are similar to those of the previous one, in that the vitamin was administered for too short a time. Prolonged dosing with the vitamin C could have had a more profound action on the length of time taken to recover from a cold.

Males and females are different in the way they handle vitamin C that is given to them. This is the conclusion of Professor C. Wilson of the University of Dublin after studying the cold-prevention effect of the vitamin in boys and girls. After giving either 200 or 500mg of ascorbic acid or a placebo to boys and girls he found, surprisingly, that the girls attained higher blood levels of the vitamin than did the boys. When given placebo the girls tended to develop colds of longer duration than the boys but the boys' symptoms were more complex. When girls received vitamin C, the severity and intensity of their colds was significantly reduced, even more so at the higher dose. The vitamin had less effect, albeit a significant one, on the intensity and duration of the colds that developed in the boys.

Further studies on the metabolism of vitamin C in males and females have suggested to Professor Wilson that different amounts are needed to combat colds. He has shown that vitamin C utilization increases during a cold because of its function in maintaining defence mechanisms against the virus and in promoting healing of the damaged tissues. His results suggest that 2g of ascorbic acid every six hours will maintain normal metabolic turnover of the vitamin during a cold, and that 2g daily should have a preventative effect against the common cold in 90 per cent of females. Males will require 2.5g daily as a prophylactic against infections, but once the cold is established, a similar regime to that of the female will suffice.

The two most recent studies have been carried out in South Wales. They are of interest because they too indicate differences in response between the sexes. And significantly, they show that benefit can be obtained with lower vitamin C intakes. The first was a randomized controlled trial when 399 women were given tablets containing 1000mg of ascorbic acid, one daily. The control group (349 women) were given placebo. The colds were divided into type, simple and chest, and their duration noted. There was evidence that at the end of 100 days trial period, the vitamin had a small preventative effect on chest colds, but none on the simple type. The mean duration of all the colds was the same in both treated and placebo groups.

In the second study much less vitamin C was given, only 80mg in orange juice, to 175 students of both sexes. The placebo group received an orange flavoured drink containing no ascorbic acid. After an experimental period of three months, there were 18 per cent less cold symptoms amongst those given the extra vitamin C. Moreover, among those students receiving the vitamin, men had significantly less severe colds than women.

The longest and most successful clinical trial on record is that carried out by Dr Edine Reginier of Massachusetts, U.S.A., and reported in the *Review of Allergy* (1968). He treated 22 patients for five years, using the following regime: 600mg ascorbic acid at the first sign of a cold followed by 600mg every three hours or 200mg every hour. At bedtime the amount taken is increased to 750mg. This quantity (4g per day) is continued for three or four days then reduced to 400mg every three hours for several days, further reducing to 200mg every three hours. With this regime, the vitamin C taken had bioflavonoids in addition, and of 34 colds, 31 were averted. Excellent results were also obtained with vitamin C alone when 45 out of 50 colds were averted. This method of taking vitamin C at the onset of a cold is a sensible one and it avoids the sudden discontinuation of the vitamin that was a feature of less successful trials.

One property of vitamin C that does appear to be generally accepted is that of an anti-histamine agent. A paper in the *Journal of Allergy and Clinical*

Immunology in 1973 describes how a dose of 500mg ascorbic acid inhibits the bronchospasm induced by inhaling a histamine aerosol. The sniffling, eye-watering throat tickle and nose-tingling associated with the common cold may be due to a histamine reaction in the injured tissues. This is why anti-histamine drugs are present in most popular 'cold-cure' preparations. As vitamin C is a natural substance that can have a similar effect, it could go part of the way in explaining how it may benefit in relieving the symptoms of the common cold. Perhaps it should be tried as a substitute for drug anti-histamines in other conditions like hay fever and allergic rhinitis, since it exerts its effect without inducing the drowsiness associated with these drugs.

Cancer Prevention and Treatment

It is now generally accepted that the development of a cancer is determined, to a large extent by the natural resistance of the individual to the disease. Therefore it would appear to be logical to increase one's ability to resist cancer by proper intake and utilization of the factors known to influence that resistance. There is now growing evidence that ascorbic acid is a determining factor in controlling and developing body resistance to the various agents that are known to cause cancer. We shall now consider these agents with particular reference to how ascorbic acid may act against them.

Epidemiological Evidence

Many studies have shown a definite negative correlation between the intake of vitamin C and the incidence of cancer. This simply means that the lower the amount of vitamin C eaten the more the chance of developing cancer. A typical study was made in California some 40 years ago. Those with the higher regular vitamin C intake in the diet had only 40 per cent the incidence of those with consistently low intake of the vitamin in the same age groups. Simply increasing the dietary vitamin C from 25mg per day to 125mg decreased by 60 per cent the chances of cancer. In real terms, this represents an increase in life expectancy of 11 years. This is approximately the same increase in life expectancy that can be achieved by not smoking cigarettes.

Studies on patients suffering from cancer indicate another relationship with vitamin C. They invariably have low body levels of the vitamin and the signs are that their requirements of it are much greater than those who do not have the disease. Like all epidemiological studies, these are only indicative, but they have been sufficient to stimulate much research into how vitamin C may protect against cancer and even how the vitamin may help therapeutically.

Inhibition of Nitrosamine Formation

Nitrosamines are substances that are known to be associated with increased incidence of certain cancers, particularly those of the stomach, the bladder and the oesophagus. Unfortunately, nitrosamines are readily formed from other compounds that are widely available in food, drugs, cosmetics, and the environment. One group of these is the nitrates, chemicals found in many vegetables and in drinking water. Nitrates as such are less dangerous than nitrites which are readily formed from them. Bacteria easily convert nitrates to nitrites and the latter are also added to cured meats, bacon, sausages and the like. Nitrites are excellent preserving agents which is why they are added to foods. However, although nitrites have some inherent toxicity, particularly to babies, it is their property of reacting with amines, substances also naturally available that results in production of the carcinogenic substances, nitrosamines.

Experiments suggest that neither nitrites nor amines

will cause cancer alone but their interaction is deadly. All of us are constantly eating nitrites and amines, yet not everyone succumbs to cancer, so there must be a natural protecting agent present. This is ascorbic acid, which competes with the amines for the nitrite present. As long as there is sufficient vitamin C present in the diet, nitrites are harmlessly detoxicated.

The ratio of the concentration of ascorbic acid to nitrite is important in determining the effectiveness of preventing formation of nitrosamines. Under simulated gastric conditions, a ratio of 1 to 1 provides 37 per cent protection; 2 to 1 gives 74 per cent and 4 to 1 protects to the extent of 93 per cent. The quantities of nitrite compared with ascorbic acid in the diet are relatively small, so a good intake of vitamin C daily, when taken with the food, will ensure complete in-activation of the nitrites. Amines are not confined to food and also appear in medicinal drugs and cosmetics, so reaction with nitrites can take place any-where. Ample vitamin C within the body will protect against nitrosamine formation whenever it takes place.

Vitamin C appears to have another function in this respect by actually combining with and detoxifying the nitrosamine after it has been formed. It is possible that the vitamin interferes also with the way in which nitro-samines cause cancer. This suggestion has been put forward by Dr J. A. Edgar of the Division of Animal Health in Melbourne, Australia. He points out that vitamin C is essential for the protein-making machinery that makes cells function properly. Nitro-samines disrupt this machinery and cause growth far beyond the normal, which is the basis of cancer. By inactivating the nitrosamines, ascorbic acid ensures that the control of cell growth is normalized. Only adequate vitamin intake will provide the necessary concentration to achieve this.

Any condition that reduces the amount of stomach acid appears to potentiate the formation of nitrosamines. Lack of stomach acid is known as achlorhydria and it is a feature of several diseases, including pernicious anaemia. Excessive acid production in the stomach is under the control of the vagus nerve and the operation known as vagotomy, which is simply cutting the nerve is undertaken to curb the flow of acid. Partial removal of the stomach is often necessary in some gastric complaints and this too leads to a lack of acid in that organ. All of these patients who lack stomach acid are more prone to form nitrosamines. At the same time they also show a higher incidence of gastric cancer. The best protective agent against nitrosamines is ascorbic acid and it would appear to be a logical step for these people to ensure a high intake of this vitamin.

Other carcinogenic (cancer-producing) substances can be produced within the body. Bladder cancer, for example can result from the conversion of the amino acid L-tryptophan to 5-hydroxyanthranilic acid. Neither compound will induce cancer, but 5-hydroxyanthranilic acid may be further converted to a carcinogen. This later conversion is prevented by ascorbic acid. Linus Pauling claims that the excess vitamin C that appears in the urine and faeces after a high oral intake is in itself protective. There is a certain amount of logic in this. Vitamin C in the urine could prevent the conversion of 5-hydroxyanthranilic acid to the carcinogenic substance in the bladder. The quantity in the gastro-intestinal tract would be available to inactivate any carcinogens introduced with the food. It would also protect against bowel cancer, by inhibiting the carcinogenic compounds that may be produced by the known interaction of food constituents as they move along the intestinal tract.

Resisting Cancer Growth
The consistent feature of any cancerous growth is the way that cancer cells are able to proliferate and

infiltrate into surrounding tissues, completely out of control of normal body mechanisms. Any resistance that can be applied by the host depends on its ability to encapsulate that growing tumour and prevent its further spread. It follows therefore that the stronger the normal body tissues are, the more likely they will resist the malignant growth. It is common knowledge that invasive tumour cells prefer to spread along the soft tissues and are deflected or constrained by the tougher areas of the body.

The main barrier to the progress of the cancer therefore is the collagen network. If this is strong and resistant, the growth will be encapsulated within it. If it is weak then the tumour cells will dissolve it and continue their proliferation.

What evidence do we have of the importance of collagen resistance? This is provided by the measurement of urinary hydroxyproline levels. It will be recalled that the amino acid, hydroxyproline is a unique constituent of collagen. Very little is eaten in the food and most of that required for collagen synthesis is produced by the body from the other amino acid called proline. Hence, the hydroxyproline in the urine can only come from the destruction of collagen. When this destruction is excessive as in cancer, urinary hydroxyproline increases and is a good measure of the extent of the cancerous growth. For example, it has been shown by Professor J. W. T. Dickerson and his colleagues at the University of Surrey that urinary hydroxyproline levels in patients with breast cancer are directly proportional to the spread of the disease. Even more intriguing, the higher the excretion of hydroxyproline, the lower are the white blood cell levels of ascorbic acid. When these ascorbic acid levels were increased by giving 1g of the vitamin per day, the excretion of hydroxyproline decreased dramatically.

It is now well established that patients with malignant disease have minimal tissue stores of vitamin C and may show the symptoms associated with subclinical scurvy. These patients also have increased requirements for the vitamin. Those with rapidly spreading cancers use twice as much vitamin C as those with slow growth or normal controls.

When these observations are taken into account with those on hydroxyproline excretion, it is possible to hypothesize that in this situation we have all the ingredients for a weakened collagen resistance to the spread of the tumour. If we can strengthen that collagen with ample vitamin C, it is reasonable to suppose that encapsulation of the growing tumour is more likely to occur.

Similar results have been observed on patients with bone tumours. When these people were treated with 1g of ascorbic acid three times daily, there was a similar dramatic reduction of hydroxyproline excretion. Of more direct benefit to the patient however, was the relief of bone pain with these high levels of vitamin C.

Immunity to Cancer
We have seen that once a cancerous growth starts, it is important that the body has efficient mechanisms for its containment and prevention of further spread. If this can happen, it makes surgical removal easier or allows the body itself to dispose of the growth. Immunity however, is the ability of the body's defence mechanisms to prevent the tumour forming in the first place. This ability is called immunocompetence and it is well known that those actually suffering from cancer have decreased immunocompetence when measured by standard tests. Also, patients maintained on longterm drugs known as immunosuppressants have an increased incidence of certain forms of cancer, presumably due to destruction of their own immune systems by the drugs.

The white blood cells responsible for immunity are the lymphocytes and their competence in this function is determined by their ascorbic acid content. For example, guinea-pigs that are maintained on diets devoid of vitamin C are able to accept and retain organs transplanted from other guinea-pigs. This indicates that their immunity is low. When they were fed sufficient vitamin C to saturate their lymphocytes, all the transplanted organs were promptly rejected showing that their immunocompetence had been restored. Dr R. H. Yonemoto of the City of Hope National Medical Centre, Duarte, U.S.A. confirmed these findings in human beings. When 5g ascorbic acid per day was fed to healthy young subjects, their immunocompetence increased as their lymphocyte level of the vitamin increased. Giving the higher dose of 10g ascorbic acid per day enhanced their immunocompetence even further.

Cancer patients have low vitamin C status and much decreased immunocompetence. The simplest and safest way to enhance their immunocompetence is to ensure that their defence mechanisms, mediated through the lymphocytes are working at maximum efficiency. This is best done with adequate vitamin C intake, sufficient both to satisfy their increased requirements and to saturate the white blood cells. Those who wish to strengthen their own resistance to cancer would also be wise to aim for a daily intake of vitamin C to saturate their body tissues.

Antiviral Activity
Some cancers are thought to be initiated by viruses and we have seen that there is some evidence that ascorbic acid acts as a preventative against the common cold — a disease caused by viruses. The effectiveness of vitamin C in inactivating the virus causing poliomyelitis was reported as long ago as 1935 by Dr C. W. Jungeblut of Columbia University. Other microorganisms that succumb to the vitamin are herpes virus, vaccinia virus, hepatitis virus and many others.

Most of these studies were carried out on isolated viruses in the laboratory, but when monkeys were treated with vitamin C, then challenged with the virus, a high degree of protection was developed by the animal. To reach and maintain in human blood the sort of concentration of vitamin C necessary to inactivate the viruses, would require intravenous injection of 20g of the vitamin, reported Dr A. Muraton et al, in 1971. Poliomyelitis patients have been successfully treated with large amounts of ascorbic acid by Dr F. R. Klemner, a physician of North Carolina, U.S.A. The injected doses were very high at a level of 400 to 600mg per kilogram of body weight; this means that a 70kg (11 stone) individual would receive 28 to 42g every eight or twelve hours.

Dr F. Morishige and his colleagues at Fukuoka General Hospital, Japan reported on the effectiveness of vitamin C in the prevention and treatment of various viral diseases in 1978. His prime concern was the prevention of post-surgical hepatitis in a country where this disease is common. By giving his patients 2g of ascorbic acid per day he reported complete success in over 1000 patients. Less intake than this produced some success, but it was by no means complete. Other viral diseases that were successfully contained by vitamin C treatment included measles, mumps, orchitis, viral pneumonia, shingles and viral encephalitis.

The exact mechanism whereby vitamin C acts against viruses is not known. It can enhance interferon production and we know that this material is the body's own antiviral agent. Recent, rather premature, publicity has claimed that interferon may be an anticancer treatment for some patients. If this turns out to be so, it could confirm that it is simply by-passing the mechanism, whereby increasing their ascorbic acid intake would in fact stimulate the body's own production of interferon. The true situation of course, is likely to be far more complicated than this. What is without doubt is that there is ample evidence that viruses can be overcome by vitamin C. We have seen also that the phagocytic (engulfing) properties of white blood cells are enhanced by vitamin C and this mechanism could also act against viruses. Hence, if some cancers are due to viruses, and the only way to prove this is to isolate these viruses, it is almost certain that ascorbic acid will be found to have a preventive and therapeutic effect against them.

Therapeutic Action Against Cancer
Although ascorbic acid has been shown to be effective against some artificially produced cancers in mice, rats and guinea-pigs, there are very few clinical trials in man. The most comprehensive was that reported by Dr Ewan Cameron from the Vale of Leven Hospital in Scotland. He treated 100 advanced cancer patients with 10g of ascorbic acid per day (given as sodium ascorbate), and reported that they felt better, had more energy, had better appetites and in some cases suffered much less pain. In a few cases their tumours shrank and in a very small proportion the growths disappeared. The most promising result was an in-creased average survival time of 293 days. A similar group of advanced cancer patients, who had not received vitamin C treatment had an average survival time of only 38 days. The results, though not outstanding were promising.

A similar study was therefore undertaken by the Mayo Clinic in Rochester, Minnesota, U.S.A. These researchers reported in the *New England Journal of Medicine* (1979) that they had treated 60 advanced cancer patients with 10g of vitamin C per day, given as 20 tablets of 500mg each. A comparative group of 63 patients of the same type and stage of cancer, age and sex were given milk sugar tablets to act as a placebo. There was no difference in survival time of the two groups. About 80 per cent of the patients in each group were dead three months after the study began. All but one of the 123 patients were dead within eight months and the one left alive was taking placebo tablets. Even the improvements in symptoms were similar, 63 per cent of this category taking vitamin C and 58 per cent on milk sugar tablets.

The main difference between the two trials was that the patients in Scotland had not received the strong immunosuppressive drugs that those in U.S.A. had been treated with. Dr Linus Pauling believes this may explain the different responses. He suggests that as the vitamin enhances the body's natural immunity to cancer so its effects would be weaker in advanced cancer patients whose immunity is thought to be impaired. Nor would its effects be as great in those who had received previous strong immunosuppressive drugs and radiation treatment, both of which suppress immunity.

There the matter rests at the moment. It would be a brave doctor who would be prepared to withhold all conventional anti-cancer treatment and rely upon vitamin C only. The patients in both trials were terminal cancer cases and it would be argued that earlier treatment with vitamin C would provide greater benefit. A recent study from Japan has given essentially the same results as those from the Scottish trial. Patients in both these studies had received some conventional treatment, but were not treated with the same strong immunosuppressive drugs that the American patients received, because they were not available to them. A second study is promised from the Mayo Clinic, only this time they will choose patients who have not been treated with the strong drugs. It will be interesting to see if they confirm the promising results obtained elsewhere.

CHAPTER 6

OTHER ASPECTS OF THE VITAMIN

Whenever vitamin C appears in foods it is always accompanied by the bioflavonoids. Hence, when Dr Albert Szent-Gyorgi was isolating ascorbic acid from citrus fruits and paprika he also came across some highly coloured pigments which he named vitamin P. Vitamin P turned out to be a mixture of chemically-related substances that had a common biological effect, so the vitamin designation was dropped and they were given the name bioflavonoids.

The bioflavonoids are a large group of substances and include commonly known compounds like rutin, hesperidin and quercetin with the equally important, but less familiar compounds nobiletin, tangeretin, sinensetin, heptamethoxyflavone and eriodictyol. In citrus fruits, the richest source of the bioflavonoids is the white pith and the core that runs down the middle of the fruit. Green peppers, which you may recall are rich sources of vitamin C also supply generous quantities of the bioflavonoids. The connection between ascorbic acid and the bioflavonoids is not just that they occur together in nature. They appear also to have a combined function in maintaining the integrity of blood vessels, particularly the blood capillaries.

Why are healthy capillaries so important? To answer this we need to look at their function. The capillaries are the ultimate blood vessels of the circulation system. They are narrow and thin-walled and because of this they are also permeable to certain constituents of the blood. Fluid from the capillaries is allowed to flow outward where it exchanges with the fluid surrounding all body cells. Hence oxygen and cell nutrients like glucose and fatty acids, minerals and

vitamins are transferred from the blood to the cells that
need them. Waste products flow back from the cells to
the far end of the capillaries which all join up and
converge into a vein. The blood cells and the plasma
proteins are selectively retained by the capillary wall
since it is the presence of these substances in the blood
that create the pressure that enables cell fluid to flow
back into the capillary. The pressure required to push
liquid out of the capillaries is provided by the heart.
Both vitamin C and the bioflavonoids are needed to
keep the capillary wall in a healthy condition that
allows the selective permeability of nutrient
substances. In the absence of these vitamins the system
breaks down, allowing the passage of whole blood into
the tissues.

Small haemorrhages under the skin are one of the
signs of scurvy because vitamin C has a recognized role
in maintaining capillary health. Lack of the vitamin
causes increased capillary fragility so that they are no
longer able to stand up to the pressure imposed upon
them. The consequence is a seepage of blood into the
surrounding tissues, resulting in what we call a bruise.
Easy bruising is another symptom of vitamin C deficiency. The colour changes that occur in bruises are
simply due to the sequence of pigments that are
produced by the breakdown of the red haemoglobin.
However, the increased permeability of capillaries that
also accompanies these changes in vitamin C deficiency is almost certainly due to a lack of bioflavonoids. As both vitamin C and vitamin P occur in
food together, it is not surprising that a deficient
dietary intake of ascorbic acid must be accompanied
by a lower intake of the bioflavonoids. Similarly, if one
is taking supplemental vitamin C, it would appear to
be a logical move also to take bioflavonoids with it.
After all, nature supplies both together.

In medicine, bioflavonoids, usually accompanied by
vitamin C, have been used for a number of complaints

associated with the blood circulation system. In France, Dr T. Muller and his colleagues at the Hospice Civils, Strasbourg have used bioflavonoids on women suffering from functional uterine bleeding. These women complained of irregular or painful menstrual flow and 90 per cent of them responded favourably to the bioflavonoid treatment. This success rate is comparable to the more conventional hormone therapy and has less side-effects. According to the report as published, the bioflavonoids functioned by improving the vein tone and increasing capillary wall resistance, i.e. strengthening them.

Other conditions that have been helped by bioflavonoids and vitamin C are varicose veins, varicose ulcers (which are the usual consequence) and haemorrhoids. Dr B. A. D. Wissmer was one of the pioneers in treating these conditions with bioflavonoids and vitamin C. He reported in *Current Therapeutic Research* (1963) that the pain and bleeding associated with haemorrhoids had stopped after two to five days treatment. The pain and swelling sensations associated with varicose veins and varicose ulcers disappeared after administering the two vitamins, but full recovery was slow and not always complete.

Some people always seem to bruise easily and when they compete in contact sports the result can often be disfiguring and painful. Dr T. F. Dowd reported in the *Science News Letter* (1959) that he had controlled bruising in professional football players by the simple expedient of supplementing them with just bioflavonoids. These were obtained from citrus fruits and a total daily dose of 300mg was given. Perhaps not many of us will suffer bruising to this extent but the first line of defence would appear to be bioflavonoids to strengthen the capillary walls. The treatment is simple, effective and safe.

One of the more life-saving aspects of bioflavonoids could be their anti-thrombosis property, according to

Dr R. C. Robbins of the University of Florida. He first demonstrated this in laboratory studies, but these have now been extended to animals and human beings. Blood contains a natural anti-thrombosis agent known as heparin, which the body makes itself. On a weight for weight basis, Dr Robbins found that nobiletin, a bioflavonoid isolated from citrus fruits, was as active as heparin in its anti-thrombotic activity in laboratory tests. When tried on rats, where the formation of thrombi was a problem, the nobiletin was just as active in the intact animal as heparin.

It would be attractive to extend these studies to human beings but no one has done so yet. The bioflavonoids could be expected to help prevent the formation of vein thrombosis which is the most worrying complication of varicose veins. What we do know is that medicine continues to use bioflavonoids in treating habitual and threatened abortion, post-birth bleeding, nosebleed, easy bruising, bleeding gums, haemorrhoids and menstrual disorders. One problem of bioflavonoids is their relatively low solubility in water, which means that they are not absorbed to any great extent. This has been overcome by a simple chemical reaction that converts the bioflavonoids to a more soluble form. The result is a medical preparation, which is widely used throughout the world as a recognized treatment for varicose veins.

Dr Robbins is one of the world's leading researchers on bioflavonoids and in a recent review (September 1980) in *Executive Health* he summed up present-day knowledge of the bioflavonoids. Apparently only a few of the many bioflavonoids that appear in nature have a distinct biochemical action — the others are clinically useless. The most potent belong to the class known as methoxylated bioflavonoids, which occur almost exclusively in citrus fruits. Hence, the anti-inflammatory property of citrus bioflavonoids resides in the fraction containing nobiletin. The anti-adhesive action on red blood cells and platelets, which prevents the formation of blood clots and thus is protective against heart attacks and strokes, is connected with a group of methoxylated bioflavonoids. Both nobiletin and tangeretin are methoxylated bioflavonoids and they can stimulate body enzymes, which in turn detoxify carcinogenic substances within the body. This particular group of methoxylated bioflavonoids possess antibacterial and antiviral properties.

The second class of bioflavonoids are known as hydroxylated and these too appear to have some specific clinical properties. Quercetin, myricetin and kaempferol have been shown in preliminary experiments to have an action in preventing formation of cataracts in the eyes. These hydroxylated bioflavonoids are natural antioxidants that act as pre-servatives in foods. Rutin, which is also a hydroxylated bioflavonoid has been claimed to be effective in treat-ing high blood pressure, arteriosclerosis, and sub-cutaneous haemorrhages due to increased capillary permeability.

The evidence suggests therefore, that to obtain the full benefit of bioflavonoids, the whole spectrum of the active members must be taken in the diet. No single bioflavonoid can exert every biochemical or physiological effect upon the body systems. Foods that are rich in these constituents are citrus fruits, apricots, cherries, grapes, green peppers, tomatoes, broccoli and buckwheat. Ample supplies of these foods in our diets will not only supply adequate bioflavonoids but also the ascorbic acid that is needed to obtain full benefit from them.

How Safe is Vitamin C?

Ascorbic acid is generally recognized as one of the safer vitamins when taken in massive doses, but there are some reports of toxic reactions from it. They include a corrosive effect upon the mouth and teeth; gastro-intestinal distress such as nausea, abdominal cramps and diarrhoea; urinary burning and frequency and, very rarely, skin rashes. These are the signs that can be noted by an individual. In addition, it is alleged that excessive vitamin C can cause metabolic disturbances, resulting in destruction of vitamin B_{12}, formation of kidney stones, inhibition of oral blood anticoagulants and an increase in uric acid excretion. A mutagenic (cell changing) effect has also been attributed to the vitamin. We shall look at each of these side-effects in turn, determine the possible contribution of vitamin C and assess the real danger of toxicity.

Gastro-intestinal Upsets

Like the possible effect of vitamin C upon the mouth and enamel of the teeth, gastro-intestinal upsets may be caused by the acidic nature of the vitamin. At low intakes of the vitamin, the contribution of acid is small and the digestive system can cope with it. When one or more grams are taken at one time some sensitive people may find that the high local concentration of acid, produced when the tablet or crystals dissolve, can produce a burning effect, particularly when taken on an empty stomach.

The remedies are thus quite simple. High concentrations of ascorbic acid can be made to bypass the mouth and teeth by taking tablets or capsules that are coated with protein or are in the prolonged release form. Food has a natural buffering or neutralizing action, so wherever possible take vitamin C with a meal. If this is not possible, as for example, in taking hourly doses to prevent or treat a cold, it is best to take the vitamin along with a little bicarbonate of soda. This remedy works by creating sodium ascorbate which has all the vitamin attributes of the ascorbic acid but none of the acidity. Alternatively, the vitamin is available as sodium ascorbate and calcium ascorbate, both of which are neutralized or buffered ascorbic acid. Most people of course are able to tolerate many grams of the vitamin as ascorbic acid quite happily, but there is no doubt that those prone to mouth ulcers or who suffer from peptic ulcers would benefit from taking the buffered variety. Urinary burning, which again is a very rare occurrence can be obviated in the same way. Chewable forms of the vitamin can also be beneficial since the acid is diluted with saliva and presented to the stomach in a weaker and hence less acid form.

The extreme tolerance to high doses of vitamin C can be illustrated by two examples. Dr H. L. Newbold in his book *Vitamin C against Cancer* (published by Stein and Day, New York, 1979) quoted the case of a patient who tried to commit suicide by taking oral ascorbic acid. After a dose of 150 grams the man merely complained of nausea and diarrhoea. In the *Medical Times* (1955), Dr E. Greer reported that he had treated five poliomyelitis patients with daily oral doses of between 50g and 80g for six to ten days. The only adverse symptoms were slight attacks of gastro-enteritis and irritation of the anus. The laxative effect of high dose ascorbic acid has been used with good effect in some cases of non-persistent constipation.

Destruction of Vitamin B_{12}

It has been noted in laboratory test-tube experiments that vitamin C as ascorbic acid had a destructive effect on vitamin B_{12}. The studies were then repeated by measuring B_{12} in food, adding pure vitamin C in excess to the food, homogenizing it and incubating the mixture for a few hours at body temperature before re-assaying the B_{12} level. The results seemed to suggest that after incubation with ascorbic acid, the concentration of the other vitamin, B_{12}, dropped dramatically. These studies were carried out some years ago, shortly after vitamin B_{12} was discovered. Modern knowledge about the techniques used then, suggested that the assay of the B_{12} was a poor one and the extraction procedures used to concentrate the vitamin were inefficient.

Consequently, the studies were repeated by Dr U. Moser from Basle, Switzerland and reported at the Vitamin C Symposium held at Warwick University in 1981. This time a more specific and sensitive assay of vitamin B_{12} was used, both before and after incubation of the food with 500mg vitamin C. There was no loss of the B_{12} vitamin. Further confirmation of the fallacy that ascorbic acid destroys vitamin B_{12} came from studies on human volunteers. Four of them were given 4g of ascorbic acid per day for a period of eleven months. Constant monitoring of their plasma vitamin B_{12} levels revealed that they did not decrease. Neither were there any clinical signs of vitamin B_{12} deficiency.

Formation of Kidney Stones

Most kidney stones are composed of the mineral calcium and oxalic acid which combine to produce calcium oxalate. They are formed when the individual has an abnormal calcium metabolism which induces high calcium excretion. At the same time, these people produce excessive amounts of oxalic acid due to some metabolic upset, or ingest large amounts from foods rich in oxalic acid. The net result is the formation of insoluble calcium oxalate which builds up gradually in the kidney to produce a stone.

When ascorbic acid is metabolized in the body, the products include oxalic acid. Hence, it has been suggested that increased ascorbic acid intake will lead to higher oxalic acid excretion, so making the possibility of kidney stone formation more likely. The fallacy of this argument has been proved by measuring the excretion of oxalate (from oxalic acid) in the urine of volunteers taking high doses of ascorbic acid.

The studies were reported by Drs W. F. Korner and

F. Weber in *Intern. Z, Vit, Ern. Forschung* (1972) and Drs D. Hornig and U. Moser at the Vitamin C Symposium (1981) at Warwick University. The normal excretion of oxalate is 35mg per day. The critical level at which stone formation would be expected to occur is 300 to 400mg per day. A total of 51 subjects were given 4g of ascorbic acid daily for four weeks and there was no significant increase in oxalate excretion over the norm. When the daily intake was stepped up to 9g per day the oxalate increase over the normal excretion averaged only 68mg, giving a total of 95mg in these subjects. This figure is far removed from the minimum critical level of 300mg per day in the urine.

Longer term studies from Japan were reported by Dr H. Takiguchi in 1966. He gave 30 healthy volunteers daily oral doses of ascorbic acid of 1 or 2g per day for between 90 and 180 days. The excretion of oxalate which amounted to between 29.3 and 29.8mg per day before supplementation with ascorbic acid did not increase even at this prolonged administration. It was only when daily doses of 8 or 9g were given that any increased excretion of oxalate took place and this was never more than 98mg daily. In all cases, once vitamin C supplementation ceased, oxalate excretion returned to normal.

These studies were of course carried out on healthy volunteers. What happens if someone already suffering from kidney stones receives high-dose vitamin C? In the study reported in 1981, four patients who were suffering from an inherited genetic disease leading to kidney stones were given 500mg ascorbic acid twice a day over two periods, four days and seven days. In all cases the oxalate excretion increased from their usual 58mg to 478 and 622mg respectively. Such a dramatic response would be expected as a result of the inherited metabolic defect in these patients. They are not able to handle ascorbic acid in the same way as a normal person. Such cases are rare, but obviously these people should be aware of the possible consequences of high ascorbic acid intakes. Anyone who knows that they have kidney stones should therefore take high doses of ascorbic acid with caution.

On the other hand, if an individual is known to be excreting large amounts of oxalic acid it does not always follow that they will form kidney stones. In these people, vitamin C taken at the rate of 1g or 2g per day does not cause an increase in the urinary oxalate levels. Oxalate can be obtained from foodstuffs other than vitamin C and an excessive amount of these in the diet will give a greater contribution to the urinary content of oxalic acid.

Perhaps Dr J. D. White reporting in the *New England Journal of Medicine* (1981) best sums up the situation. He writes: 'Although high-dose vitamin C has been implicated in calcium oxalate deposition in the kidneys of uremic patients (i.e. those with poor kidney function), it is becoming apparent that patients with normal renal (i.e. kidney) function can tolerate exceptionally high doses of this vitamin.' He quotes the case of a young man who took 15g of vitamin C daily for more than four months and maintained a perfectly normal kidney function. At the same time, it must be realized that if an individual is known to have kidney disease it is unwise to take high ascorbic acid supplements without clinical advice.

The Effect on Blood Coagulation

One of the manifestations of scurvy is an impairment in the production of blood coagulation factors, particularly in the small white blood cells known as platelets. These are the cells that bind together under normal circumstances to produce a thrombus, sealing off damaged blood vessels. Ascorbic acid may therefore be regarded as an essential factor for normal blood coagulation. Studies reported in *Klin. Med.* (1958) by Drs S. G. Aptekar and K. M. Lorie indicated that in both men and rabbits there is a reduction in the blood coagulation time after high doses of vitamin C. In the guinea-pig however, giving the vitamin does not affect the coagulation time of the blood, although the time for which capillaries bleed is shortened.

Those who are being treated with anticoagulant drugs should not take excessive doses of ascorbic acid. For example, vitamin C is known to interfere with anti-coagulant drugs of the dicoumarol type, and may partly abolish its inhibition of blood coagulation. Con-versely, Dr R. Hume and his colleagues reported in the *Journal of the American Medical Association* (1972) that they gave 1g of vitamin C per day for 14 days to five patients on long term treatment with the drug warfarin and found no effect upon the blood coagulation time. The sensible approach by anyone being treated with anticoagulant drugs is to restrict their vitamin C supplementation to a maximum of 500mg per day, unless advised otherwise by their doctors.

Other Alleged Toxic Actions
An occasional report has filtered into the medical press about the possible 'rebound' effect of high-dose ascorbic acid. What it means is that someone who takes regular high intakes of the vitamin and then stops suddenly may show some minor pre-scurvy symptoms associated with deficiency. The body apparently has learned to tolerate high blood levels of the vitamin C and eventually becomes dependent upon them. The simplest way to prevent the 'rebound' effect is therefore to ensure that when there is a desire to reduce the intake, for example following high dosage taking during illness, this is carried out gradually. There is no reason why people should not wean themselves off high dosage vitamin C over a period of weeks. Similar regimes are carried out with other vitamins and some drugs, and vitamin C is no exception. It must be pointed out however, that the number of 'rebound'

victims that have actually been reported is very low indeed. Studies aimed at producing the 'rebound' effect in experimental guinea-pigs have all produced negative results.

A recent criticism in *Nature* (1976) aimed at ascorbic acid was that, in excess it can produce mutagenic or cell-changing effects in microorganisms and animals. The experiments were carried out on isolated cells in cultures so there was no evidence presented that these effects applied to intact animals. More recent studies that were reported at the Vitamin C Symposium in 1981 have shown that ascorbic acid alone, in the systems used by the *Nature* researchers has no mutagenic action. In the presence of copper and oxygen however, evidence of a mild mutagenic action appeared. In the intact animal however, with or without copper, ascorbic acid demonstrated no mutagenic action. In fact, the Food and Drug Administration of America who authorized the later studies have concluded that vitamin C is not mutagenic.

Finally, there have been reports that one of the toxic reactions induced by a dose of between 4g and 8g per day of ascorbic acid is a higher excretion of uric acid. Uric acid may give rise to some types of kidney stones in the same way that oxalic acid does, although uric acid stones are relatively rare. This however, is one of these cases where a possible side-effect is far outweighed by a more probable benefit. High levels of uric acid in the blood can give rise to gout in some susceptible people. Treatment of the condition is therefore aimed at reducing the blood levels of uric acid and one way to do this is to stimulate its excretion. Vitamin C does exactly that, and studies have shown that 8g per day for the relatively short period of eight days reduced blood uric acid by 30 per cent. These are preliminary, but further studies are being undertaken to determine whether the blood uric acid can be decreased permanently by more prolonged administration of lower vitamin C intakes.

INDEX